First Computing Social Responsibility Workshop (CSR-NLP I 2022)

Held at LREC 2022

Marseille, France
20 – 25 June 2022

Editors:

Mingyu Wan
Chu-Ren Huang

ISBN: 978-1-7138-6116-4

Printed from e-media with permission by:

Curran Associates, Inc.
57 Morehouse Lane
Red Hook, NY 12571

CURRAN ASSOCIATES INC. proceedings.com

Some format issues inherent in the e-media version may also appear in this print version.

Association for Computational Linguistics
209 N. Eighth Street
Stroudsburg, Pennsylvania 18360

Phone: 1-570-476-8006
Fax: 1-570-476-0860

acl@aclweb.org

Additional copies of this publication are available from:

Curran Associates, Inc.
57 Morehouse Lane
Red Hook, NY 12571 USA
Phone: 845-758-0400
Fax: 845-758-2633
Email: curran@proceedings.com
Web: www.proceedings.com

LREC 2022 Workshop
Language Resources and Evaluation Conference
20-25 June 2022

The First Computing Social Responsibility Workshop (CSR-NLP I 2022)

PROCEEDINGS

Editors:
Mingyu Wan & Chu-Ren Huang

Proceedings of the LREC 2022 workshop on The First Computing Social Responsibility Workshop –NLP Approaches to Corporate Social Responsibilities (CSR-NLP I 2022)

Edited by:
Mingyu Wan & Chu-Ren Huang

For more information:
European Language Resources Association (ELRA)
9 rue des Cordelières
75013, Paris
France
http://www.elra.info
Email: lrec@elda.org

Message from the General Chair

This volume documents the Proceedings of the first Workshop on Corporate Social Responsibility (CSR) using NLP methods, held on 25 June 2022 as part of the LREC 2022 conference (International Conference on Language Resources and Evaluation. This workshop is a very first attempt of bridging data resources, language theories, and NLP technologies on CSR in particular. It has called for innovative and practical NLP methods for tackling the CSR/ESG challenges at the cross-disciplinary research, especially with the nowadays' big data language technologies. This very first volume has finally included 8 excellent papers (5 oral presentations + 3 posters) on some core topics pertaining to CSR/ESG.

Message from the Program Chairs

Corporate Social Responsibility (CSR) as a shared grand challenge in business studies and in computational linguistics has not been tackled yet in the recently thriving financial NLP studies. These work so far have been more driven by the NLP downstream technology instead of the theoretical or real-world issues driving studies of economics or business.

Conventional methods usually focus on shared values of companies such as sustainability, carbon footprint, diversity and inclusion, fair-trade, social justice, environmental impact. However, different businesses may breed additional and more specific areas of issues to address, such as pollution/emission, pharmacovigilance, food safety etc.

The goal of the workshop is to identify and develop niche research methodologies that are highly competitive and world-leading for CSR modelling. Tackling the grand challenges of the world by promoting mutual understanding through language and CSR is a necessary step towards tackling other grand challenges that also may be aided by language big data, deep neural networks, linguistic tools and methods, towards some of the trending issues in CSR studies such as environmental degradation and the climate crisis.

In CSR-NLP I 2022, we have provided such a venue for researchers and practitioners worldwide to conduct computational linguistic research and make use of NLP methods to address some of the core issues for CSR or ESG related research. We look forward to more submissions and participation in the next event, hopefully to build up large-scale CSR data resources, tools, or platforms with NLP-facilitated technologies, as well as the language resource evaluation, and to launch a shared task for CSR modeling/prediction for open competition. We believe with this considerable outcome and fruitful discussions for the first computing workshop on CSR, there will be more promising and cheerful results in the next events.

Organizers

Kathleen Ahrens – The Hong Kong Polytechnic University
Emmanuele Chersoni – The Hong Kong Polytechnic University
Chu-Ren Huang – The Hong Kong Polytechnic University
Huyen Nguyen Thi Minh – VNU University of Science
Cindy Sing Bik Ngai – The Hong Kong Polytechnic University
Weiwei Sun – Cambridge University
Rachel Edita O. Roxas – National University, Manila, Philippines
Qi Su – Peking University
Mingyu Wan – The Hong Kong Polytechnic University
Qiang Wu – The Hong Kong Polytechnic University

Program Committee:

Xiaopeng Bai (ECNU)
Maria Bonnafous-Boucher (Novancia Business School)
Jason Chang (National Tsing Hua University)
Chung-Chi Chen (AI Research Center, Japan)
Hsin-Hsi Chen (National Taiwan)
Agnes Cheng (Oklahoma State)
Emmanuele Chersoni (HK PolyU)
Chris Cieri (LDC-UPenn)
Jinghang Gu (HK PolyU)
Shu-kai Hsieh (National Taiwan)
Yu-yin Hsu (HK PolyU)
Ngyun Thi Minh Hyuen (Vietnam National)
Chunyu Kit (CityU HK)
John Lee (CityU HK)
Jing Li (HK PolyU)
Karl Neergaard (University of Macau)
Cindy Sing Bik Ngai (HK PolyU)
Bo Peng (HK PolyU)
Rachel Roxas (National U-Philippnes)
Enrico Santus (Bayer)
Qi Su (Peking U)
Mingyu Wan (HK PolyU)
Qiang Wu (HK PolyU)
Rong Xiang (HK PolyU)
Winnie Zeng (HK PolyU)

Sponsors

The workshop is substantially supported by the funding for Projects of Strategic Importance of The Hong Kong Polytechnic University (Project Code: ZE2J, Project title: Artificial Intelligence and Applications of Natural language processing in Business) and sponsored by the Research Centre for Professional Communication in English (RCPCE).

Table of Contents

Conference Program

14:00–15:00 Roundtable discussion by PC members and CSR/ESG experts

15:05–18:00 Oral Presentations

15:05–15:30 *An NLP Approach for the Analysis of Global Reporting Initiative Indexes from Corporate Sustainability Reports*
Marco Polignano, Nicola Bellantuono, Francesco Paolo Lagrasta, Sergio Caputo, Pierpaolo Pontrandolfo and Giovanni Semeraro

15:35–16:00 *Tracking Changes in ESG Representation: Initial Investigations in UK Annual Reports*
Matthew Purver, Matej Martinc, Riste Ichev, Igor Lončarski, Katarina Sitar Šuštar, Aljoša Valentinčič and Senja Pollak

16:00–16:30 Coffee break

16:35–17:00 *A Corpus-based Study of Corporate Image Represented in Corporate Social Responsibility Report: A Case Study of China Mobile and Vodafone*
Xing Chen and Liang Xu

17:05–17:30 *Framing Legitimacy in CSR: A Corpus of Chinese and American Petroleum Company CSR Reports and Preliminary Analysis*
Jieyu Chen, Kathleen Ahrens and Chu-Ren Huang

17:35–18:00 *MobASA: Corpus for Aspect-based Sentiment Analysis and Social Inclusion in the Mobility Domain*
Aleksandra Gabryszak and Philippe Thomas

18:05–18:45 Poster presentations

18:05–18:15 *Detecting Violation of Human Rights via Social Media*
Yash Pilankar, Rejwanul Haque, Mohammed Hasanuzzaman, Paul Stynes and Pramod Pathak

18:20–18:30 *Inclusion in CSR Reports: The Lens from a Data-Driven Machine Learning Model*
Lu Lu, Jinghang Gu and Chu-Ren Huang

18:35–18:45 *Towards Classification of Legal Pharmaceutical Text using GAN-BERT*
Tapan Auti, Rajdeep Sarkar, Bernardo Stearns, Atul Kr. Ojha, Arindam Paul, Michaela Comerford, Jay Megaro, John Mariano, Vall Herard and John P. McCrae

Proceedings of CSR-NLP I @LREC 2022, pages 1–8
Marseille, 25 June 2022

An NLP Approach for the Analysis of Global Reporting Initiative Indexes from Corporate Sustainability Reports

Marco Polignano §, Nicola Bellantuono °, Francesco Paolo Lagrasta *, Sergio Caputo §, Pierpaolo Pontrandolfo *, Giovanni Semeraro §
§University of Bari Aldo Moro, °University of Foggia *Polytechnic of Bari
§Dept. Computer Science *Dept. Mechanics, Matemathics and Management, Via E. Orabona 4, 70125, Bari
° Dept. of Agriculture, Food, Natural Resources and Engineering, Via Napoli 25, 71122, Foggia
{marco.polignano, giovanni.semeraro}@uniba.it
nicola.bellantuono@unifg.it
s.caputo34@studenti.uniba.it
{francescopaolo.lagrasta, pierpaolo.pontrandolfo}@poliba.it

Abstract

Sustainability reporting has become an annual requirement in many countries and for certain types of companies. Sustainability reports inform stakeholders about companies' commitment to sustainable development and their economic, social, and environmental sustainability practices. However, the fact that norms and standards allow a certain discretion to be adopted by drafting organizations makes such reports hardly comparable in terms of layout, disclosures, key performance indicators (KPIs), and so on. In this work, we present a system based on natural language processing and information extraction techniques to retrieve relevant information from sustainability reports, compliant with the Global Reporting Initiative Standards, written in Italian and English language. Specifically, the system is able to identify references to the various sustainability topics discussed by the reports: on which page of the document those references have been found, the context of each reference, and if it is mentioned positively or negatively. The output of the system has been then evaluated against a ground truth obtained through a manual annotation process on 134 reports. Experimental outcomes highlight the affordability of the approach for improving sustainability disclosures, accessibility, and transparency, thus empowering stakeholders to conduct further analysis and considerations.

Keywords: Natural Language Processing, Information Extraction, Sustainability Reporting, Global Reporting Initiative, Corporate Analysis

1. Introduction

The EU Corporate Sustainability Reporting Directive (CSRD), proposed on April 21, 2021[1], would significantly extend the scope of sustainability reporting legislation among European companies. With a stated aim of bringing sustainability reporting on a par with financial reporting, it would help to have equal weight and rigor. The currently in force Non-Financial Reporting Directive applies to some large companies operating in the EU. CSRD would extend the reporting obligation to all large companies, either listed or unlisted, as well as to all listed firms, with the sole exception of listed micro-companies. The reporting obligation would also be extended to all groups, which will have to produce a consolidated sustainability report. Estimates predict that the application of these new inclusion criteria will bring the number of sustainability reporting obliged companies from the current 11,700 to about 49,000.

The ways in which companies approach sustainability reporting are often varied and non-standard. While society and governments demand sustainable development, the efforts deployed by companies are often not adequate. Only recently, given the numerous initiatives towards environmental and social respect, some of the largest and best-known companies have decided to accept the request of national and supranational governments for more adequate reporting on these issues (Bowen, 2014). Nonetheless, economics still play a pivotal role for environmental decisions, and according to (Dyllick and Muff, 2016), companies' understanding of sustainability has been misguided resulting in most companies committed to reducing unsustainability rather than actually pursuing sustainability. Identifying relevant sustainability topics and disclosing related information seems then a quite challenging task even for responsible companies, resulting in lower communication efficacy and in turn accessibility by stakeholders (e.g. consumers, authorities). The identified issues to some extent depend on the difficulties in monitoring activities experienced by the competent bodies: sustainability reports are often complex, with customized layouts, long, and challenging to read, which make their analysis time consuming and costly. We propose to address such issues by means of the support of computer systems. We developed an approach based on Natural Language Processing (NLP) and Information Retrieval (IR) to support the review process of such documents. Our system is capable of analyzing documents in closed format, i.e., PDF, and

[1] https://ec.europa.eu/info/business-economy-euro/companyreportingandauditing/company-reporting/corporatesustainabilityreporting_en

extracting information potentially valuable for the review phase. In fact, referring to the Global Reporting Initiative (GRI) Standards[2], we searched for sustainability topics in the textual document in order to identify the context of use and the page where they are discussed. Our approach speeds up the operations of analysis, study, and review of corporate documents on sustainability.

1.1. Research Goals

In this work, we aim to address the issue of automatic analysis of textual documents concerning sustainability. In particular, we want to investigate the possibility of adopting NLP and IR techniques to be able to automatically extract relevant information for possible consultation and review by stakeholders. Specifically, it was considered that the preliminary analysis that could be done is to check whether specific sustainability topics or disclosures are discussed in the document. In this work, we focus on sustainability reports compliant with GRI Standards as the latter are by far the most widely adopted. This task, which might seem simple, is instead made complex by the heterogeneity of layouts and the writing style of sustainability documents. We believe that an automated system capable of detecting which topics are actually discussed within the sustainability reports could be a valuable aid for stakeholders as well as anyone involved in the process of reviewing corporate documents. The main contributions of this work are:

- An NLP and IR strategy for the automatic analysis of corporate sustainability reports;
- A system to automatically analyze GRI Standards compliant reports;
- An evaluation using real reports that focuses on GRI topics/disclosures and on the analysis of the extracted contexts.

2. Related Work

Describing how an organization deals with its economic, environmental, and social impacts is an articulated process, called sustainability reporting, whose deliverable is nowadays usually defined as sustainability report. Although the early attempts to describe social activities of companies date back to the 1970s whereas companies involved in environmentally sensitive industries began to publish their environmental reports in the subsequent decade, only in the mid-1990s the first periodic reports of activities, encompassing the three sustainability dimensions in a holistic perspective, were published. These reports, which at the beginning were almost entirely limited to bigger companies, timidly spread also among SMEs, institutions and no profit organizations (Hsu et al., 2013).

More recently, the rapid increase of awareness on the responsibility that businesses play to achieve sustainable development shed a new light on the practice of sustainability reporting (Minutiello and Tettamanzi, 2022). Sustainability reports, indeed, become crucial for companies not only to communicate to stakeholders how they deal with sustainability, but also to reflect on their sustainable strategies and embrace them committedly. Reporting, in fact, "is not only a matter of communication nor a mere data gathering or compliance exercise. It helps organizations to set goals, measure performance, and manage change" (Global Reporting Initiative, 2013). Recent norms and initiatives on the compulsory release of non-financial disclosures have put a new emphasis on studies of sustainability reporting. Scholars, in particular, have investigated the plethora of schemes proposed to help report sustainability (Grewal and Serafeim, 2020), which often let companies discretionarily choose the shape to adopt for their reports, the content included and the way to identify and present it, at the price of making reports hardly comparable, so weakening the general audience's ability to retrieve information they need. Even when companies strictly follow the Global Reporting Intiative standards, which act as a de facto standard for sustainability reporting, they release heterogeneous kinds of documents, which hinder the identification of resemblances and dissimilarities among companies' sustainability strategies, priorities, and results.

Therefore sustainability reports are configured as complex sources, adopting non-standard layouts and different methods of information representation (e.g. text, tables, infographics), in which both unstructured and semi-structured data can be traced. This feature, combined with the amount of documentation produced annually by companies from all over the world, makes the investigation of sustainability reports through NLP and Text Mining (TM) techniques an interesting and potentially vastly impacting scientific challenge (Zhou et al., 2021). As a matter of fact, NLP techniques allow to analyze and automatically represent texts written in human languages to obtain a human-like language processing useful for subsequent analysis (Liddy, 2001). TM provides instead automatic processes aimed at extracting implicit knowledge from textual data (Jo, 2019), enabling inferences otherwise impractical for the human reader.

Companies non-financial disclosures have been investigated using NLP and TM techniques starting from 2009, when Bayesian analysis and TM were used to measure report content differences among multiple sectors (Modapothala and Issac, 2009). Since then, such techniques have been adopted to investigate different aspects related to non-financial documentation. In (Aureli et al., 2016) TM was used to assess changes in the quantity of sustainability disclosures delivered by companies before and after an industrial disaster. Changes over time were also tracked in (Székely

[2]https://www.globalreporting.org/standards/

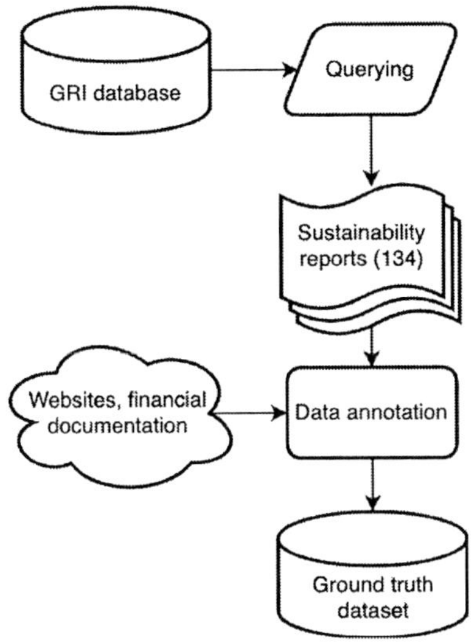

Figure 1: Ground truth dataset creation process.

and vom Brocke, 2017) where authors performed latent Dirichlet allocation (LDA, an NLP technique for topic modeling) to record the evolution over the span of 16 years (1999 - 2015) of the topics contained within sustainability reports. (Lindgren et al., 2021) adopted Bayesian machine learning and LDA, arguing that shareholders appear to be the implicit target users of sustainability reports. (Zhou et al., 2021) used LDA to explore container shipping companies sustainability disclosures. It is not an isolated case: many of the studies focusing on the application of NLP and TM on sustainability reports are devoted to specific industries in order to identify sector-dependent characteristics, trends and best practices (e.g. (Wang et al., 2020), (Uyar et al., 2021)).
This brief overview of the literature contributes to demonstrate how the use of these techniques could prolifically support the investigation of sustainability reports. Despite the research stream boasting a history of more than ten years, to the authors' knowledge, no study was aimed at developing tools intended for the sustainability disclosures (e.g., GRI Standards) information retrieval.

3. Resources and Annotation Process

The dataset used as ground truth to test the effectiveness of the developed tool contains data extracted from 134 sustainability reports, retrieved from the online GRI Sustainability Disclosure Database[3] in March 2021. Fig. 1 depicts the dataset creation process.

[3]Unfortunately GRI decommissioned the Sustainability Disclosure Database, which is no longer accessible. More information is available at https://www.globalreporting.org/how-to-use-the-gri-standards/register-your-report/

The reports were selected through a query that returned GRI Standards compliant documents published by Italian companies: for each of them, the latest available report was included in the dataset. The query design ensures homogeneity in terms of framework (GRI Standards) and national culture (Italian). On the other hand, no constraints were imposed on the size and sectors of the drafting companies: hence, the dataset contains reports ascribable to 27 different sectors (e.g. waste management, automotive, agriculture) published by micro (2/134), small (2/134), medium (4/134) and large (126/134) organizations. The unbalanced representation with respect to the drafting organizations size is due to the previously mentioned European norms, which state that non-financial disclosures are mandatory for large companies.
After report selection, the dataset was populated. Each report underwent a manual annotation phase aimed at structuring organizational, financial and sustainability-related data. The annotation process involved two researchers: the first populated the dataset while the second performed spot checks on the correctness of the information entered. The wide scope of the selected features allows the dataset to be leveraged as a knowledge base for testing new hypotheses and/or developing tools with a potentially different purpose than that of this work. The following organizational and financial variables related to the drafting companies were selected: company name, sector, number of employees, size, annual turnover and annual balance sheet total. As these data were not always contained within the reports, they were collected from different data sources, such as drafting companies websites and miscellaneous financial documentation. In order to collect data pertaining to sustainability-related aspects, we manually scanned the documents in full, extracting title, year, language, reporting option (GRI Standards allow two options - core or comprehensive- to be chosen), involved stakeholders, stakeholder engagement strategy and GRI disclosures. GRI disclosures were recorded through a dummy variables approach: each disclosure-related feature was valued 1 (yes) if it had been included in the report and 0 (no) otherwise. The resulting dataset contains 134 reports published by as many Italian companies. Each report is described by 150 features, 108 of whom are related to GRI sustainability disclosures.

4. The Natural Language Processing Pipeline

Most of the corporate sustainability reports are organized into five main sections, including management information, environment, and climate change, environmental performance review, a listing of verifiable environmental claims and green initiatives, and declarations about environmental compliance. In addition, information about the internal organization's structure, the departments responsible, and employees' roles in

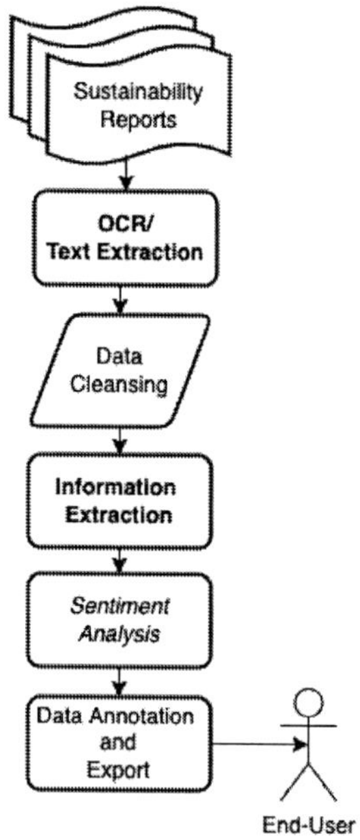

Figure 2: NLP Pipeline for processing the Sustainability Reports.

sustainability activities are provided in most reports. However, companies are not forced to use a predefined standard in the layout design of reports: different design choices are taken for characters style, sections design, and disposition, graphs, images, number of pages, etc.
In order to correctly analyze the documents of our dataset, we decided to implement a complete NLP pipeline (Fig. 2). The first step is the conversion of sustainability reports into a computable textual format. Considering the format of files in the dataset, we had to convert each PDF file into a set of images that could be processed by an OCR (Optical Character Recognition) tool to extract a textual representation of the pages a report consists of. The extracted text is consequently the starting point to perform a focused search on GRI disclosures presence. Before starting the process, we had to make a suitable input for the OCR tool. For this purpose, we used Poppler[4], a library for rendering PDF files and examining or modifying their structure. It was used to convert PDF reports into a collection of images, in which each image corresponded to a page in the report. Then, we adopted Tesseract (Smith, 2007), an OCR engine able to convert the text contained into an image obtained with scans, pictures, or photos into understandable characters for a word processor. The results are usually excellent as far as character recognition is concerned. Conversely, it lacks the ability to maintain page layout, particularly when tables or columns occur in the document. Initially limited to ASCII characters, since March 2022 Tesseract supports UTF-8 characters and recognizes more than 100 languages[5]. During this transformation step, in many cases we observed that the resulting text was not accurate enough to be considered a robust mapping of the content discernible by a human observer. This issue is mainly caused by the need to transform the document pages into images before applying the OCR tools. For this reason, we decided to enrich the textual representation we obtained with text extracted directly from the PDF format. For this purpose, PDFplumber[6] was exploited. It is a Python open-source package whose objective is directed to parsing PDFs, analyzing PDF layouts and object positioning, and extracting text. For our case, we used this library to extract text directly from PDF.

Intending to improve the quality of the text obtained using the two approaches, we decided to apply classical text cleaning techniques. In particular, we decided to remove stopwords as well as to replace carriage returns, tab characters, double or triple spaces with single spaces. In addition, we decided to remove every non-alphanumeric character and/or character of length less than or equal to two, including punctuation, except for the "-" character because it is used within the notation of GRI disclosures. We performed this task using the Spacy Library (Srinivasa-Desikan, 2018). In particular, it provides a complex text analysis pipeline for several languages, including Italian. It offers the possibility of dividing the text into tokens and checking if each of them is a stopword, its length, and the type of content.

Given the textual representation of the reports, we were able to perform a keyword search based on common GRI Standards' disclosures names in order to estimate the presence and absence of them within the document. The conversion of each PDF page into searchable textual content also allowed us to detect the portion of text where each of the GRI standard disclosure was located in the analyzed document. In particular, we can extract the page number and the paragraph containing the GRI Standards' disclosures names. We searched for 215 total keywords created by using the following two possible structures: "GRI <code>", "<code>". The element <code> is an integer number referring to GRI topics between 200 and 400 or their disclosures like 200-x, 300-x, and 400-x. Keywords like "GRI 300-4" or "GRI 203" or "306-4" are examples of of used search terms. Limitations of this approach include the possibility of identifying any numerical values in sustainability reports as GRI topics/disclosures. To overcome that limit, we decided to evaluate a second version of our search pipeline which makes use only of keywords obtained by using GRI disclosures, i.e., those containing the "-" symbol. This makes the pos-

[4] https://pypi.org/project/python-poppler/

[5] https://github.com/tesseract-ocr/tesseract

[6] https://github.com/jsvine/pdfplumber

sibility of false positives very unlikely. In that second approach, we considered a match for a GRI Standard if at least one of its disclosures was identified in the text. In both cases, we considered as the reference context of the specific GRI standard, the portion of the text that contains it, i.e., the one obtained by extracting the 25 terms before and after the match. As an output of this step of the proposed pipeline, we are able to obtain the possible match for each of the possible GRI topics, the reference context, and the page of the document where the match has been identified. This output can be exported for later use by the end-user or optionally processed through a sentiment analysis tool.

Sustainability reports should discuss aspects relevant to the drafting organization and to its stakeholders, highlighting both positive and negative outcomes. Notwithstanding this, companies might tend to report only positive information, neglecting to inform stakeholders about negative performances (Boiral, 2013). In order to verify if this misuse is commonly applied, we can conduct an analysis that takes into account also the sentiment of the context where the GRI disclosures were found. We expect inhomogeneous sentiments since, in principle, each company should make available information, whether positive or negative, especially in the sustainability context. In the literature many approaches for Sentiment Analysis have been proposed (Polignano et al., 2017b; Polignano et al., 2017a; Polignano et al., 2019). In particular, in this work, we decide to use two tools: TextBlob[7] and Sent-It (Basile and Novielli, 2014). TextBlob is a Python library for processing textual data with common NLP tasks. It was adopted to recognize the sentiment for contexts written in English. Sent-It is a sentiment analysis tool that identifies the sentiment for Italian texts. It is a system based on a supervised machine learning approach. In particular, for training, three different kinds of features based on keywords and microblogging properties of tweets, on their representation in a distributional semantic model, and on a sentiment lexicon have been exploited. Data provided for training are annotated according to the subjectivity/objectivity of the content. Moreover, each piece of text is categorized as positive, negative, or neutral. In our case, most of the disclosure's contexts were written in Italian, and we are able to obtain a score of polarity (i.e., positive, negative) and subjectivity/objectivity.

At the end of the analysis process, it is possible to export the results of each document in JSON format. It shows the reference context (if any), page number, polarity score, and subjectivity score for each GRI disclosure. The proposed system has been coded in the Python language and run on the Google Colab Environment[8]. The source code has been released through the GitHub platform[9].

	OCR	Text Extr.	GRI	Sub GRI	Sent.
OCR -all-GRI	✓		✓		
OCR -sub-GRI	✓			✓	
TE -all-GRI		✓	✓		
TE -sub-GRI		✓		✓	
OCR-TE -all-GRI	✓	✓	✓		
OCR-TE -sub-GRI	✓	✓		✓	
OCR-TE-SA -all-GRI	✓	✓	✓		✓
OCR-TE-SA -sub-GRI	✓	✓		✓	✓

Table 1: Configurations of the system we evaluated.

5. Evaluation

The evaluation phase aims to assess the effectiveness and robustness of the proposed system. In particular, we want to investigate the following research questions:

- **RQ1:** Is it possible to develop a robust and effective system for automatically search GRI topics from corporate sustainability reports?
- **RQ2:** How system performances are influenced by the granularity chosen for the keywords used while searching for GRI standards?
- **RQ3:** How the system performances are influenced by the tool used for the text extraction from PDF files?
- **RQ4:** Is it possible to use a sentiment analysis tool for evaluating if sustainability reports are discussing only positive aspects?

With the goal of answering the research questions posed, we ran our system using different configurations. In particular, following the configurations reported in Tab. 1, we used OCR, Text Extractor, or both as document processing tools and all possible or disclosure keywords for the search phase. Finally, we evaluated two configurations based on the use of the sentiment analysis tool, for which we considered a match for the search phase, only GRI topics with a neutral or positive context.

The results obtained from the experimental runs are shown in Tab. 2. It is possible to observe that the results obtained in terms of the F1 measure are promising for all the configurations discussed. In particular, it

[7] https://textblob.readthedocs.io/en/dev/index.html

[8] https://colab.research.google.com/

[9] https://github.com/marcopoli/GRI-Sustainability-Reports-Analysis

	Precision	Recall	F1
OCR -all-GRI	*0.95579*	0.80189	0.87210
OCR -sub-GRI	0.95103	0.89208	0.92061
TE -all-GRI	0.95752	0.80704	0.87586
TE -sub-GRI	0.95228	0.89616	0.92337
OCR-TE -all-GRI	0.95577	0.84152	0.89501
OCR-TE -sub-GRI	0.95014	*0.93725*	*0.94365*
OCR-TE-SA -all-GRI	0.95642	0.79034	0.86548
OCR-TE-SA -sub-GRI	0.95106	0.87259	0.91014

Table 2: Results obtained from the evaluation runs.

varies from the lowest value of 0.87210 obtained from the OCR-all-GRI configuration to 0.94365 found by performing the OCR-TE-sub-GRI configuration. What has been observed shows that in its simplicity, the analysis pipeline presented is highly effective, allowing to obtain results that can represent an excellent base of departure for end users. It is, in fact, clear that a value of F1 measure so close to the value 1 is an indication of the effectiveness of the discovery process and the reliability of the results obtained. This allows us to answer the **RQ1** positively.

Observing the fine-grained results we obtained, in some cases, lower Recall values have been obtained with respect to the average. This issue was caused by the absence of some disclosures we used in the search phase. Indeed using the keywords about the first level of the GRI standards caused many situations of mismatching where the manual annotator has considered the first level of the GRI standard found only because one of its disclosures has been found. Similarly, we performed some configurations by using only keywords obtained from GRI disclosures and considered a match for the first level of the GRI Standard if at least one of its disclosures was identified in the text. Configurations that contain the string "-sub-GRI" in the name are those that follow this approach. What can be observed is that in all cases, these configurations behave better than their "-all-GRI" counterparts. There is, in fact, an increase in performance that varies from 5.16% to 5.56%. The results obtained allow us to provide a clear answer to **RQ2**.

To avoid as many errors as possible due to the incorrect encoding of text resulting from PDF conversion operations, configurations using different text extraction techniques were performed. The results obtained show that using a text extractor succeeds in reducing some of the problems of OCR, particularly those in which the text was shown on colored backgrounds or in fonts that are difficult to interpret. On the contrary, the text contained in images is ignored. Indeed, we moved from an F1 measure value of 0.92061 for the OCR-based technique to 0.92337 for the one based on Text Extractor. Instead, the best performances are achieved when combining approaches. A GRI standard is considered identified if it is found in the text obtained by at least one of the two approaches. This process allowed us to obtain an F1 score of 0.94365, the highest among the results of our runs. These considerations allow us to provide a response to **RQ3**.

Putting our attention to the last two configurations posted in Tab.2, OCR-TE-SA-all-GRI and OCR-TE-SA-sub-GRI, we can observe that the performance of the proposed pipeline decreased comparing them with their counterpart without sentiment analysis applied. This would suggest that in the reports, there are also contexts in which there is a negative concept expressed about a GRI standard. Unfortunately, however, following a detailed analysis, it has been observed that the negative contexts identified are false positives. In fact, they are generated by the misclassification of the same by the sentiment analysis tool used. The presence of certain negative words could definitely affect the sentiment processed using the Sent-It tool. We detect that words such as "rischi", "corruzione", "malattia", "pericoloso" could heavily influence the final sentiment prediction especially if these were found in sentences that uses negations. The results in Tab. 3, show us the most common terms in case of misclassification. These represent words in the Italian language that express, if taken individually, a negative sentiment. Conversely, their use in a negated form or with an outlined context can lead to overall positive sentiment. This shows that corporate sustainability reports tend to present only the positive goals achieved. What was observed appears to be a valid response to **RQ4**.

6. Implications of Research, Limits and Challenges

The proposed approach to analyze sustainability reports is a first step towards the possibility of offering complete and reliable support to the interested stakeholders. In fact, it is common to observe documents that use heterogeneous layouts and different writing styles, sometimes even when adopting the same reporting standard/guideline. The analysis of such documents becomes a demanding, long and tedious task. Therefore, a computer system can be an essential support for analysis operations, as long as it is reliable and effective. The approach we propose is based on a straightforward methodology. The obtained results, though limited to a single PDF format, GRI Standards, and documents written in Italian or English, prove that the approach is viable. Further research could address such limitations by extending the scope of our approach to different formats, standards, and languages. These

Root word	% False Positive OCR	% False Positive Text Extr.
rischi	0,16	0,14
corruzione	0,14	0,14
rifiuti	0,08	0,09
discriminator	0,01	0,01
malatti	0,08	0,07
inquinant	0,01	0,01
spesa	0,01	0,01
emission	0,03	0,04
infortun	0,07	0,07
sanzion	0,05	0,05
incident	0,05	0,05
decess	0,03	0,03
pericolos	0,03	0,03
violazion	0,03	0,05
mort	0,02	0,02

Table 3: Percentage of contexts erroneously classified with negative sentiment containing the root word.

points are the challenges that we will face in future work, with the aim of making the system presented here as complete and reliable as possible. The sentiment analysis strategy presented here is the basis for in-depth analysis work that could be conducted on such reports. Elements such as subjectivity, writing style, and ease of reading could prove to be interesting information to assess the quality of such documents. This could have substantial managerial implications for firms willing to become aware of the actual interest of stakeholders in their sustainability reports.

7. Conclusion

Sustainability reporting should be considered as an impartial and transparent helpful tool to explain sustainable goals, objectives, and companies' activities to their stakeholders. These reports are an excellent resource for monitoring corporate best practices that address environmental, social, and economic sustainability. However, companies often produce reports which, even when they are compliant with GRI Standards or other reporting standards, are poorly structured and thus complex to read and analyze. Therefore, in this work we addressed the problem by proposing a system supporting the analysis of sustainability reports, specifically designed to identify the topics/disclosures discussed within GRI compliant reports. We propose a system based on a pipeline of Natural Language Processing and Information retrieval able to deal with closed format files, i.e. PDFs. The documents were transformed into a machine-readable textual format using OCR and Text Extraction tools. The text obtained here has been considered as the raw data over which to perform a keyword search operation. In particular, we considered keywords representative of the GRI topics and disclosures. This approach was repeated with different configurations of the system with the aim of optimizing the search process and, consequently, the final retrieval performances. The obtained results showed that the system we proposed is extremely performant on the considered dataset, showing a score of F1 measure equal to 0.94365. It was also observed that the text extraction strategy from the PDF format could strongly impact on the obtained results, suggesting a hybrid extraction mode to make up for the shortcomings of OCR and Text Extraction tools. The search strategy can also strongly affect performance. The design of the most correct keywords to be used has in fact proved to be a fundamental step in the implementation of the system. Finally, the sentiment analysis tool proved to be a useful component of the proposed system, by demonstrating that the examined reports seem to emphasize positive aspects rather than negative ones, which would contradict one of the GRI reporting principles (balance). A key future challenge is to enhance the system in terms of robustness, efficiency, effectiveness, and flexibility.

8. Acknowledgements

The work of Marco Polignano has been supported by Apulia Region, Italy through the project "Un Assistente Dialogante Intelligente per il Monitoraggio Remoto di Pazienti" (Grant n. 10AC8FB6) in the context of "Research for Innovation - REFIN". We would like to thank Francesco Mastrorosa who developed the dataset used in this work.

9. Bibliographical References

Aureli, S., Medei, R., Supino, E., and Travaglini, C. (2016). Sustainability disclosure after a crisis: A text mining approach. *International Journal of Social Ecology and Sustainable Development (IJSESD)*, 7(1):35–49.

Basile, P. and Novielli, N. (2014). Uniba at evalita 2014-sentipolc task predicting tweet sentiment polarity combining micro-blogging, lexicon and semantic features. *UNIBA at EVALITA 2014-SENTIPOLC Task Predicting tweet sentiment polarity combining micro-blogging, lexicon and semantic features*, pages 58–63.

Boiral, O. (2013). Sustainability reports as simulacra? a counter-account of a and a+ gri reports. *Accounting, Auditing and Accountability Journal*, 26(7):1036–1071.

Bowen, F. (2014). *After greenwashing: Symbolic corporate environmentalism and society*. Cambridge University Press.

Dyllick, T. and Muff, K. (2016). Clarifying the meaning of sustainable business: Introducing a typology from business-as-usual to true business sustainability. *Organization & Environment*, 29(2):156–174.

Global Reporting Initiative. (2013). Gri-g4 sustainability reporting guidelines—reporting principles and standard disclosures 2013. `http://www.globalreporting.org/resourcelibrary/`

GRIG4-Part2-Implementation-Manual.pdf. Accessed: 2022-04-01.

Grewal, J. and Serafeim, G. (2020). Research on corporate sustainability: Review and directions for future research. *Foundations and Trends® in Accounting*, 14(2):73–127.

Hsu, C. W., Wen-Hao, L., and Wei-Chung, C. (2013). Materiality analysis model in sustainability reporting: a case study at lite-on technology corporation. *Journal of Cleaner Production*, 57:142–151.

Jo, T. (2019). Introduction. In *Text Mining: Concepts, Implementation, and Big Data Challenge*, pages 3–17. Springer International Publishing, Cham.

Liddy, E. D. (2001). Natural language processing. In *Encyclopedia of Library and Information Science*. Marcel Decker Inc., New York.

Lindgren, C., Huq, A. M., and Carling, K. (2021). Who are the intended users of csr reports? insights from a data-driven approach. *Sustainability*, 13(3).

Minutiello, V. and Tettamanzi, P. (2022). The quality of nonfinancial voluntary disclosure: A systematic literature network analysis on sustainability reporting and integrated reporting. *Corporate Social Responsibility and Environmental Management*, 29(1):1–18.

Modapothala, J. R. and Issac, B. (2009). Study of economic, environmental and social factors in sustainability reports using text mining and bayesian analysis. In *2009 IEEE Symposium on Industrial Electronics Applications*, volume 1, pages 209–214.

Polignano, M., Basile, P., Rossiello, G., de Gemmis, M., and Semeraro, G. (2017a). Learning inclination to empathy from social media footprints. In *Proceedings of the 25th Conference on User Modeling, Adaptation and Personalization*, pages 383–384.

Polignano, M., Gemmis, M. d., Narducci, F., and Semeraro, G. (2017b). Do you feel blue? detection of negative feeling from social media. In *Conference of the Italian Association for Artificial Intelligence*, pages 321–333. Springer.

Polignano, M., Basile, P., de Gemmis, M., and Semeraro, G. (2019). A comparison of word-embeddings in emotion detection from text using bilstm, cnn and self-attention. In *Adjunct Publication of the 27th Conference on User Modeling, Adaptation and Personalization*, pages 63–68.

Smith, R. (2007). An overview of the tesseract ocr engine. In *Ninth international conference on document analysis and recognition (ICDAR 2007)*, volume 2, pages 629–633. IEEE.

Srinivasa-Desikan, B. (2018). *Natural Language Processing and Computational Linguistics: A practical guide to text analysis with Python, Gensim, spaCy, and Keras*. Packt Publishing Ltd.

Székely, N. and vom Brocke, J. (2017). What can we learn from corporate sustainability reporting? deriving propositions for research and practice from over 9,500 corporate sustainability reports published between 1999 and 2015 using topic modelling technique. *PLOS ONE*, 12(4):1–27, 04.

Uyar, A., Koseoglu, M. A., Kılıç, M., and Mehraliyev, F. (2021). Thematic structure of sustainability reports of the hospitality and tourism sector: A periodical, regional, and format-based analysis. *Current Issues in Tourism*, 24(18):2602–2627.

Wang, X., Yuen, K. F., Wong, Y. D., and Li, K. X. (2020). How can the maritime industry meet sustainable development goals? an analysis of sustainability reports from the social entrepreneurship perspective. *Transportation Research Part D: Transport and Environment*, 78:102173.

Zhou, Y., Wang, X., and Yuen, K. F. (2021). Sustainability disclosure for container shipping: A text-mining approach. *Transport Policy*, 110:465–477.

10. Language Resource References

Resource Type: Corpus
Resource Name: GRI-134-IT
Size: 134 documents
Resource Production Status: Newly created-finished
Language(s): Italian
Modality: Written
Use of the Resource: Information Extraction
Resource Availability: From Owner
License: Creative Commons rights reserved 4.0 - Noncommercial - Share Alike - International
Resource URL: https://github.com/marcopoli/GRI-Sustainability-Reports-Analysis/blob/master/GRI-134-IT.csv
Resource Description: This is a corpus of corporate sustainability reports that should be compliant with the Global Reporting Initiative standards.

11. Annexes

Contribution of authors:

- Marco Polignano: writing of Sections 1, 4, 5, 6, 7, process modeling and formalization
- Nicola Bellantuono: writing Section 2 (Related works)
- Francesco Paolo Lagrasta: writing Section 3 (Resources and Annotation Process)
- Sergio Caputo: process development, execution of experiments
- Pierpaolo Pontrandolfo: conceptualization, supervision
- Giovanni Semeraro: conceptualization, supervision

Proceedings of CSR-NLP I @LREC 2022, pages 9–14
Marseille, 25 June 2022

Tracking Changes in ESG Representation: Initial Investigations in UK Annual Reports

Matthew Purver,[*‡] **Matej Martinc,**[*] **Riste Ichev,**[†] **Igor Lončarski,**[†]
Katarina Sitar Šuštar,[†] **Aljoša Valentinčič,**[†] **Senja Pollak**[*]
[*]Department of Knowledge Technologies, Jožef Stefan Institute, Ljubljana, Slovenia
[†]School of Economics and Business, University of Ljubljana, Ljubljana, Slovenia
[‡]School of Electronic Engineering and Computer Science, Queen Mary University of London, UK
{matthew.purver, matej.martinc}@ijs.si, {riste.ichev, igor.loncarski, katarina.sitar,
aljosa.valentincic}@ef.uni-lj.si, senja.pollak@ijs.si

Abstract

We describe initial work into analysing the language used around environmental, social and governance (ESG) issues in UK company annual reports. We collect a dataset of annual reports from UK FTSE350 companies over the years 2012-2019; separately, we define a categorized list of core ESG terms (single words and multi-word expressions) by combining existing lists with manual annotation. We then show that this list can be used to analyse the changes in ESG language in the dataset over time, via a combination of language modelling and distributional modelling via contextual word embeddings. Initial findings show that while ESG discussion in annual reports is becoming significantly more likely over time, the increase varies with category and with individual terms, and that some terms show noticeable changes in usage.

Keywords: environmental, social, governance, ESG, diachronic analysis

1. Introduction

Companies and investors are becoming increasingly aware of the importance of Corporate Social Responsibility (CSR) in their actions, tracking and reporting their impact on society and the environment. One way to examine a company's behaviour in this area is via Environmental, Social and Governance (ESG) criteria. ESG criteria cover a company's environmental impact (Environmental), their relationships with their community including employees, suppliers and customers (Social), and their leadership structures including executive pay, shareholder rights, audits and controls (Governance). ESG analyses are currently performed manually by experts; for example, Lydenberg et al. (2010) define a method for identifying key sustainability performance indicators which requires six detailed analysis steps. Our interest is in developing NLP technologies to help automate this process, to characterise companies in terms of different ESG criteria and understand how these relate to company performance, risk and outlook over time, as well as more general changes in the economic and regulatory environment. Given the increasing investor interest, coupled with the regulatory push in terms of non-financial reporting, mostly driven by sustainability motives, understanding of the connection between corporate ESG reporting and the measurement of ESG is becoming very important. So far, regulatory requirements regarding ESG reporting have been relatively loose. However, this is starting to change very quickly and dramatically, as exemplified by the introduction of the EU taxonomy for sustainable activities, sustainability reporting standards such as SASB, and the most recent evolution in IFRS reporting. While NLP techniques have been developed for specific aspects relating to ESG, particularly environmental concerns (Armbrust et al., 2020) and more specifically, discussion relating to climate change (Luccioni et al., 2020), a more general model for tracking and characterizing ESG reporting has yet to be produced.

In this paper, we outline our initial steps in this direction, by defining a categorised set of 93 ESG terms covering 5 core ESG areas, based on a number of existing resources and filtered by multiple annotators, that can be used to analyse changes in reporting. By assembling a collection of company annual reports and applying analyses based on language modelling and on distributional methods, we show that these terms have the potential to reveal changes in the frequency and in the usage of the language of ESG.

2. Dataset and ESG analysis terms

2.1. Data and pre-processing

We base our analysis on annual reports from FTSE350 companies over the years 2012-2019. To establish a fixed list of companies for comparison purposes, we used the FTSE350 list as of 25th April 2020.[1] Reports were obtained from the publicly accessible collection at www.annualreports.com. Not all companies' reports were available, and to disambiguate between companies with the same ticker on different exchanges, we used only those with reports shown at the London Stock Exchange (LSE); the number of reports obtained, together with total word counts (before preprocessing or

[1] `https://en.wikipedia.org/w/index.php?title=FTSE_350_Index&oldid=953125037`

Year	# Reports	# Words
2012	178	12.5M
2013	181	14.0M
2014	184	15.0M
2015	196	16.3M
2016	198	17.5M
2017	200	18.4M
2018	200	19.6M
2019	202	21.2M
total	1539	134.6M

Table 1: Number of annual reports retrieved by year

tokenization), are shown in Table 1. The reports are published as PDF documents; these were converted to raw text using the `pdf2txt` tool.[2] We tokenize into words and build ngrams of length 1-4 padded with sentence start and end symbols, using NLTK's standard preprocessing tools.[3] While we do not have the rights to redistribute this data, it comes from public sources, and the details required to re-create the dataset are available publicly at `osf.io/rqgp4`.

2.2. ESG term extraction

As our interest is in comparing the ways in which ESG concepts are written about, our first task was to define a set of suitable terms (words or multi-word expressions) for subsequent use in analysing the report text.

Initial seed terms We started with three existing lists of terms likely to relate to ESG concepts, derived from (a) the SASB standards, (b) Schroders and (c) our own work. The first list comes from the 2017 Conceptual Framework for sustainability in accounting set out by the SASB (Sustainability Accounting Standards Board, now part of the Value Reporting Foundation - see www.sasb.org): specifically, we take the "SASB Universe of Sustainability Issues" which defines 5 sub-areas (*environment, social capital, human capital, business model and innovation, leadership and governance*) and gives 4-7 major concepts for each one (SASB, 2017). For example, the concepts for *environment* include *GHG emissions, Air quality, Energy management, Fuel management, Water and wastewater management, Waste and hazardous materials management, Biodiversity impacts.* This list contains 36 terms. Our second source is the Schroders brochure "Understanding sustainable investment and ESG terms" (Schroders, 2021), used to establish "the landscape of activities, strategies that fall under the broad umbrella of ESG and sustainability", and the terms most commonly associated with each. This approach takes the point of view of the investor, and defines 6 sub-areas (*integration, governance & active ownership, screened investments, thematic investing, impact investing, industry organisations and initiatives*), each specified with 7-15 major concepts. For example, the concepts for *thematic investing* include *carbon footprint, climate risk, green investing, renewable energy.* This list contains 62 terms.

Our third and final source is an annotated dataset developed during our own project and described in (Stepišnik-Perdih et al., 2022). For this dataset, sentences were extracted from annual reports of companies listed on US or UK stock exchanges that cover the period 2017 to 2019. Annotation was then performed at the sentence level, with sentences marked as ESG-related or not. Thirteen annotators were used, with each annotator given 500 sentences for annotation. Annotators were second-year graduate students of the MSc in Quantitative Finance and Actuarial Sciences at the School of Economics and Business, University of Ljubljana. Given their field and length of studies, we believe they were well suited to the task of annotating financial texts. Annotators were asked to annotate each of the sentences according to several criteria. First, whether the sentence is relevant from the perspective of corporate business. Second, whether the sentence conveys positive/negative/neutral financial sentiment. Third, whether the sentence expresses an opinion (subjectivity) or states the facts (objectivity). Fourth, whether it is forward-looking or not. Finally, whether it relates to ESG or not. Full details are given in (Stepišnik-Perdih et al., 2022); in this work, we use only the labels with regards to ESG, with a binary label positive (ESG-related) or negative (not ESG-related). The dataset contains 6,500 sentences, within which 24.8% (1,617 sentences) are ESG-related. Based on these annotated sentences, we estimated two 1-2-gram language models using maximum likelihood estimation (using NLTK's standard language modelling tools),[4] one for ESG-related text and one for non-ESG-related text. We then extracted characteristic terms as single words or two-word terms matching the part-of-speech patterns JJ-NN* or NN*-NN* for which the ratio of the language model probabilities $p_{ESG}/p_{nonESG} > 5.0$. This list includes terms concerning a range of ESG aspects, including the environment (*greenhouse gas, meteorological parameters, ambient temperature*), social issues (*female, women, gender pay, human rights, young people, mental health*) and overall standards and reporting concepts (*ethical standard, zero harm, cultural fit, diversity policy*). This list contains 109 single-word and 233 two-word terms.

Term selection We combined these lists to give 440 candidate ESG-related terms of length 1 to 3 words. We randomly shuffled this list, and 4 annotators with finance expertise were independently asked to label each as to whether it was likely to be a representative ESG term, and if so to categorize it according to a 6-way

[2] `https://github.com/pdfminer/pdfminer.six/blob/develop/tools/pdf2txt.py`

[3] `https://www.nltk.org/api/nltk.lm.preprocessing.html`

[4] `https://www.nltk.org/api/nltk.lm.html`

1SC	social capital
2HC	human capital
3BMI	business model & innovation
4LG	leadership & governance
5E	environment
6ESG	environmental social governance

Table 2: ESG category labels, derived from the SASB Conceptual Framework (SASB, 2017)

schema shown in Table 2. The schema consists of the 5 sub-areas of ESG defined by the SASB conceptual framework (SASB, 2017), together with a sixth general category for terms that could not be categorized under any of those 5.
Inter-annotator agreement over the entire list of candidate terms was reasonable, with overall average pairwise Cohen's kappa 0.50 (minimum 0.32, maximum 0.60). Of the 440 candidate terms, 311 were given a label by at least one annotator, but only 93 were given a label by all four annotators (i.e. unanimously agreed to be representative ESG terms). We take these 93 terms as our term list for analysis. Over this set, agreement on the ESG category labels was good, with average pairwise Cohen's kappa 0.71 (minimum 0.63, maximum 0.78). We take the most frequently assigned label as the gold-standard ESG category for each term. The final term list is available publicly at `osf.io/rqgp4`.

3. Language modelling analysis

After text pre-processing, we build a language model for each year in our dataset for word ngrams length 1-4, using maximum likelihood estimation (again using NLTK's standard language modelling tools). This allows us to perform comparison across years of the probabilities of occurrence of 1-to-4-word terms, and of the most likely context following occurrences of those terms. To find terms which have changed most in their probability of use, we find the gradient over time: taking the probability of use of a term over time, we apply standard zero-mean/unit-variance scaling, fit a simple linear regression model and extract the first coefficient. We also do the same for the mean probabilities over the set of terms for each ESG category.

ESG categories We find that overall, ESG terms are becoming more likely in company reports over time, in particular since 2015/2016 annual reports: for all the 6 ESG categories, gradients are positive - see Figure 1. However, there are significant differences in the gradients, with some categories growing faster than others. The fastest-growing is *2HC human capital*, followed by *5E environment* and *3BMI business model*; the slowest-growing are *1SC social capital* and the general/other category *6ESG*.

ESG terms Individual ESG terms, on the other hand, vary widely. Some are increasing noticeably in probability, and the 10 most increasing terms include terms

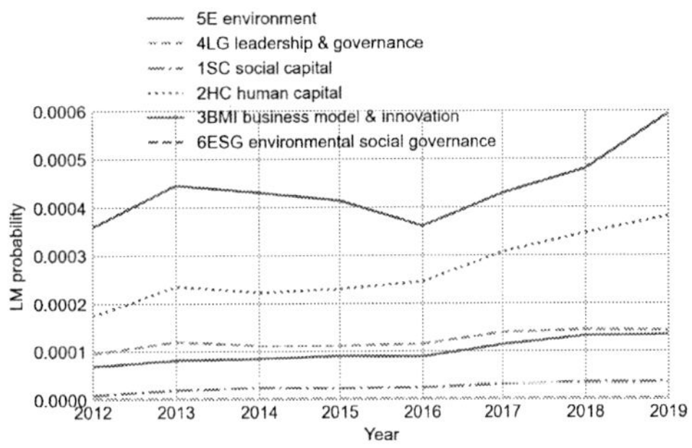

Figure 1: Average probability of mention of ESG term categories over time

from all 5 of our main ESG categories: in 1SC, *human rights*; in 2HC, *talent, wellbeing, pay gap, gender pay*; in 3BMI, *innovation*; in 4LG, *ethical, governance framework*; in 5E, *climate change, renewable.* Figure 2 shows these 10 most increasing terms. Similar to the findings related to ESG categories, terms associated with 2HC human capital exhibit some of the strongest growth in probability after 2015/2016. It also seems that the driver in the growth of 5E environment category is mostly related to the term *renewable*.

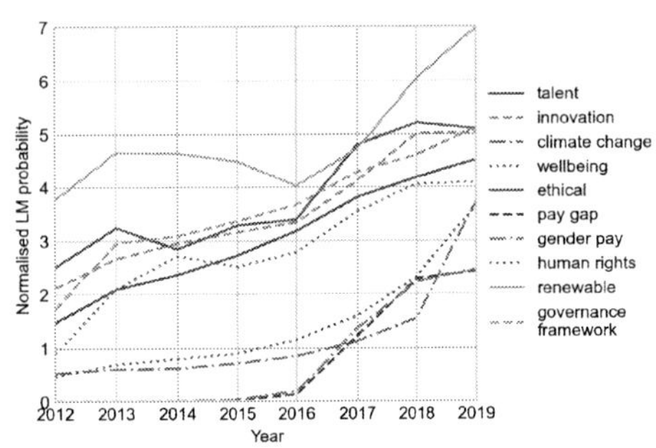

Figure 2: Probability of mention of 10 most increasing ESG term categories over time

Many other terms, though, are increasing more slowly, and some are decreasing in probability. Figure 3 shows the 10 most decreasing terms: *compensation, corporate responsibility, environmental management, waste management, pension plan, water treatment, human resources, emission control, compliance committee, business ethics*. Again, most categories are represented (with the exception of 1SC, social capital), but the nature of the terms is different. In 2HC (human capital), the emphasis now seems less on equality (*pay gap, gender pay*) and on individuals (*talent, wellbeing*) and more on general issues (*human resources*) and on financial aspects (*compensation, pension plan*). In 5E (environment), the emphasis now seems less on specific issues and more on policies and compliance. This

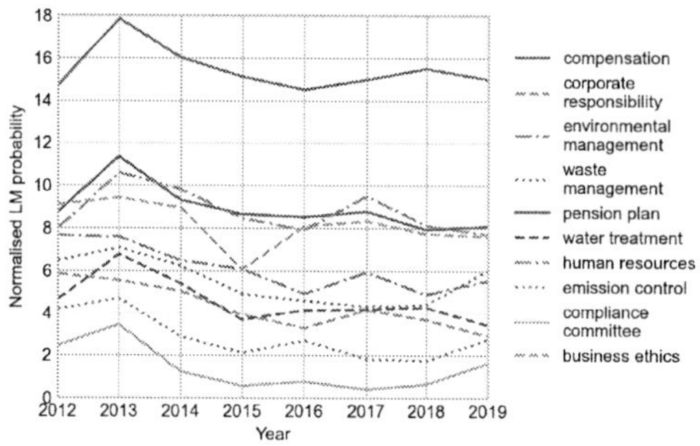

Figure 3: Probability of mention of 10 most decreasing ESG term categories over time

therefore seems to have potential to reveal some finer-grained changes over time in the discussion of ESG and the emphasis placed on certain aspects; however, it seems likely that our 6 general ESG categories — and therefore taxonomies such as the SASB Conceptual Framework from which they were taken — may not be fine-grained enough to analyse this quantitatively, and could benefit from more detailed subcategorization to allow direct analysis.

4. Contextual analysis

Given this, we next turn to look at whether these terms have changed in usage over time, as well as frequency: changing likelihood of use of a term may simply indicate a straightforward change in its frequency of use in reporting, but may also be associated with changes in the context of its use, as it becomes used in different ways or with different emphases. One possible way to examine this is again through language modelling, by inspecting changes in the most likely continuations predicted by a language model after observing a term.[5] However, for the terms of interest here, we find few differences: likely continuations are dominated by syntactic dependencies and end-of-sentence predictions.

Instead, we applied a distributional method used in our previous work to examine diachronic changes in word usage (Montariol et al., 2021). For each word, we generate a set of contextual word embeddings using BERT (Devlin et al., 2019), summing over sub-word tokens where required. These vector representations are then clustered using k-means (taking the clusters to approximate fine-grained word senses), and the resulting cluster distributions compared across years. We measure distance between distributions using Jensen-Shannon divergence (JSD) (Lin, 1991), and take this as a measure of the relative degree of usage shift.

Overall degree of change This allows us to rank our ESG terms by their degree of usage shift over time. The most changing terms (those with the biggest overall distance between distributions from 2012 to 2019) include many terms whose likelihood increased most in the analysis of the previous section (e.g. *wellbeing, talent*); as well as other terms with only moderate likelihood increase (e.g. *pollution, greenhouse gas*). Interestingly, though, some of the terms whose usage changed least (those with the smallest overall distance from 2012 to 2019) also include terms whose likelihood increased sharply (e.g. *innovation, human rights*). Figure 4 shows how JSD varies across time for some selected terms which show high degrees of usage change (*wellbeing, talent, pollution, greenhouse gas*) together with some which show low change (*environmental, innovation*). Erratic and significant year-to-year changes for individual terms might be idiosyncratic. For example, a significant increase for the term *pollution* between 2013 and 2015 might be related to a particular industry and/or single major environmental disaster. The usage of the term *innovation* changed by a factor of 10 less than the usage of the term *wellbeing*; although the likelihood increase (probability gradient) of *innovation* was 50% higher than that of *wellbeing*.

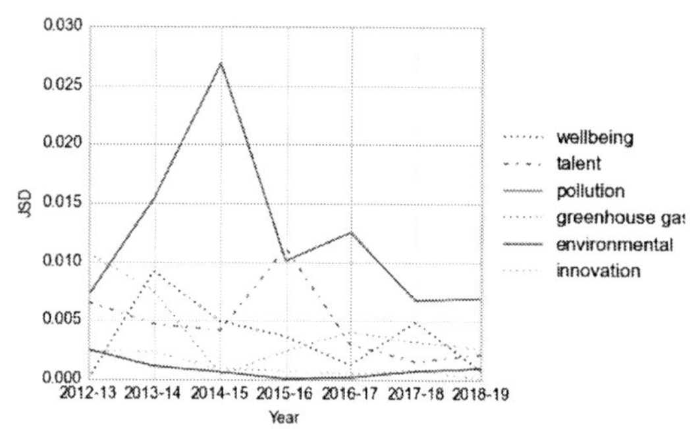

Figure 4: Jensen-Shannon divergences between adjacent year pairs over time, for selected high-change and low-change terms

Cluster analysis For terms which show high usage change, this raises the question of in what ways the usage has changed. A full investigation must be approached qualitatively, in order to understand what themes are emerging or being reduced; but we can gain some insight by examining which of the sense clusters become more or less frequent. Figure 5 shows the cluster distributions (proportions of sentences assigned to each cluster by k-means) over time for two high-change terms (*talent, wellbeing*) and two low-change terms (*environmental, innovation*). For each cluster, we show a set of representative keywords: these are extracted by finding those with the highest tf-idf score when considering a cluster as a single document and all clusters as a corpus, while excluding stopwords and words appearing in over 80% of clusters.

Taking one example, we can inspect the term *wellbe-*

[5] Manual analysis and coding may allow deeper insights in future when time allows, see e.g. (Burgers and Ahrens, 2018).

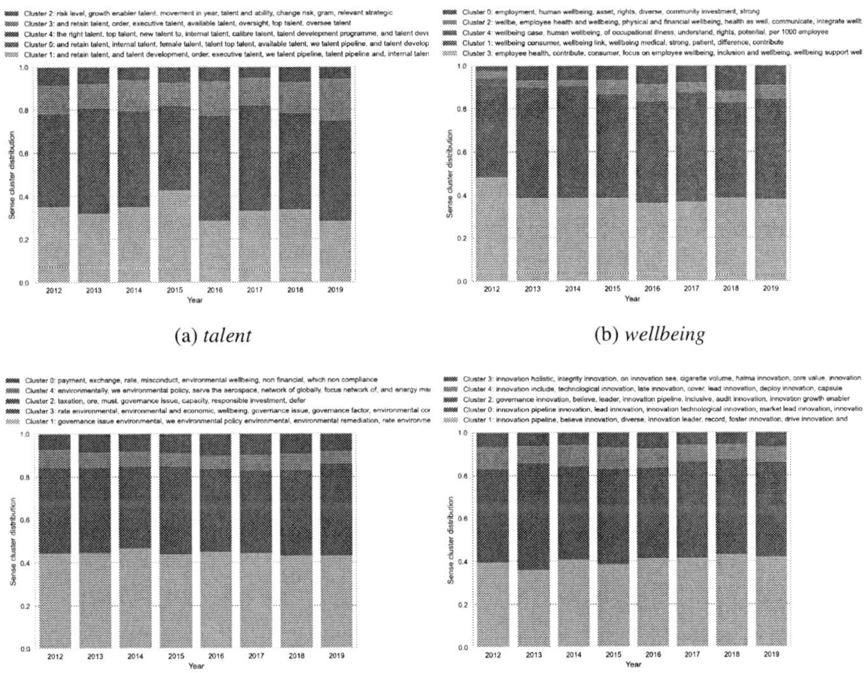

(a) *talent* (b) *wellbeing*

(c) *environmental* (d) *innovation*

Figure 5: Cluster distributions over time for four selected ESG terms: (a),(b) show two terms whose distributions change most, and (c),(d) show two terms whose distributions change least

ing (Figure 5(b)), and see that sense cluster 3 decreases noticeably in likelihood over time, while clusters 0 and 2 increase. The extracted keywords themselves give some limited insight into the differences: the increasing clusters 0 and 2 include keywords relating to *diversity, community* and *financial wellbeing*; however there is also a significant amount of overlap, with *employee wellbeing* and *employee health* seemingly covered in both increasing and decreasing senses. Manual inspection of sentences assigned to particular clusters gives some more insight, with sense cluster 3 (decreasing) seeming to be more focused on general statements of values, while clusters 0 and 2 (increasing) are more specific. Cluster 0 contains a high proportion of concrete statements of past actions, while cluster 2 contains more focused statements about health and financial aspects of wellbeing. Table 3 shows some (manually chosen) examples.

Acknowledgements

The authors acknowledge the financial support from the Slovenian Research Agency for research core funding (No. P2-0103 and No. P5-0161), as well as for funding of the research project *Quantitative and qualitative analysis of the unregulated corporate financial reporting* (No. J5-2554).

5. Bibliographical References

Armbrust, F., Schäfer, H., and Klinger, R. (2020). A computational analysis of financial and environmental narratives within financial reports and its value for investors. In *Proceedings of the 1st Joint Workshop on Financial Narrative Processing and MultiLing Financial Summarisation*, pages 181–194.

Burgers, C. and Ahrens, K. (2018). Change in Metaphorical Framing: Metaphors of TRade in 225 Years of State of the Union Addresses (1790–2014). *Applied Linguistics*, 41(2):260–279, 12.

Devlin, J., Chang, M.-W., Lee, K., and Toutanova, K. (2019). BERT: Pre-training of deep bidirectional transformers for language understanding. In *Proceedings of the North American Chapter of the Association for Computational Linguistics: Human Language Technologies*, pages 4171–4186.

Lin, J. (1991). Divergence measures based on the shannon entropy. *IEEE Transactions on Information Theory*, 37(1):145–151.

Luccioni, A., Baylor, E., and Duchêne, N. A. (2020). Analyzing sustainability reports using natural language processing. *ArXiv*, abs/2011.08073.

Lydenberg, S., Rogers, J., and Wood, D. (2010). From transparency to performance: Industry-based sustainability reporting on key issues. Technical report, Hauser Center for Nonprofit Organizations at Harvard University. Available

0	Health and wellbeing: During the year, the Committee reviewed the significant amount of work being undertaken across the Group as we continue to promote, support and deliver a multitude of health and wellbeing activities for employees, comprising a mix of physical, mental and occupational services.
0	As a Board, we are satisfied that there is no complacency in the business with regards to health and safety but we will continue to challenge the leadership team to maintain a constant focus on the safety of our colleagues and customers and their health and wellbeing, particularly in areas where some risk inevitably arises such as driving within our predominantly route based businesses, and working at height.
0	As a result, over 90% of leaders feel that they are comfortable having conversations about mental health with their team peers and managers, know about and are comfortable signposting colleagues to the resources available to them • 4,000 colleagues have taken advantage of the free access to Headspace offered, collectively completing over 66,000 sessions since launch Physical wellbeing • 8% of colleagues have taken advantage of our discounted fitness proposition which launched in 2018, and they've certainly been active, clocking up over 31,000 gym visits, and the equivalent of 970 days worth of exercise!
0	The year also saw us launch a Wellbeing Programme encouraging open dialogue through monthly presentations on a range of health topics including healthy eating, drugs awareness, emotional well-being and cancer; making sure our people are aware of additional supporting information and the free health and wellness resources available such as flu jabs, eye tests and general physical wellbeing checks.
2	Health and wellbeing initiatives have been selected locally and include well person clinics, office fruit baskets and exercise classes.
2	We have health and wellbeing champions across the business globally and this year they have organised and promoted a range of health and wellbeing activities in our offices, from informative briefing sessions on healthy living through to massage sessions.
2	Nearly four in five employees believe that [ANON] values their health and wellbeing, up nine percentage points in 2017 alone following the launch of a highly successful Health and Wellbeing programme.
2	Financial and health wellbeing is top of employer agendas and we continue to support them and their employees with further development of [ANON] Wellbeing, a set of services aimed at helping employers build healthier, happier and more productive workforces.
3	By inspiring and enabling people to never stop growing and take charge of their wellbeing Unlock capacity for growth
3	Our purpose statement, which was developed in partnership with colleagues from across the business is to be the local partner taking care of journeys that enhance the lives and wellbeing of our communities across the world.
3	Cultivating community spirit and wellbeing in [ANON] Middle-East with [ANON] Sports.
3	The wellbeing of everyone who interacts with our business is a top priority for [ANON].
3	Our beautiful homes, passionate people and excellent wellbeing services set the scene for the creation our communities.

Table 3: Example sentences with k-means cluster labels for the term *wellbeing*

from https://iri.hks.harvard.edu/links/transparency-performance-industry-based-sustainability-reporting-key-issues.

Montariol, S., Martinc, M., and Pivovarova, L. (2021). Scalable and interpretable semantic change detection. In *Proceedings of the North American Chapter of the Association for Computational Linguistics: Human Language Technologies*, pages 4642–4652.

SASB. (2017). SASB conceptual framework. Technical report, Sustainability Accounting Standards Board, San Francisco, CA, February. Available from https://www.sasb.org/wp-content/uploads/2020/02/SASB_Conceptual-Framework_WATERMARK.pdf.

Schroders. (2021). Understanding sustainable investment and ESG terms. Technical report, Schroder Investment Management Limited, London, UK. Available from https://www.schroders.com/de/sysglobalassets/global-assets/english/campaign/sustainability/interpret/understanding-sustainable-investment-and-esg-terms.pdf.

Stepišnik-Perdih, T., Pelicon, A., Škrlj, B., Žnidaršič, M., Lončarski, I., and Pollak, S. (2022). Sentiment classification by incorporating background knowledge from financial ontologies. In *Proceedings of the 4th Financial Narrative Processing Workshop*.

Proceedings of CSR-NLP I @LREC 2022, pages 15–23
Marseille, 25 June 2022

A Corpus-based Study of Corporate Image Represented in Corporate Social Responsibility Report: A Case Study of China Mobile and Vodafone

Xing Chen[1], Liang Xu[*1, 2]
Jiangxi Agricultural University, Xi'an Jiaotong University
1. No. 1101 Zhimin Avenue, Nanchang, Jiangxi, 330045, P.R.C.
2. No. 28 Xianning West Road, Xi'an, Shaanxi, 710049, P. R.C.
cx762021@163.com, ndxuliang@163.com

Abstract

By examination of the high-frequency nouns, verbs, and keywords, the present study probes into the similarities and differences of corporate images represented in Corporate Social Responsibility (CSR) reports of China Mobile and Vodafone. The results suggest that: 1) both China Mobile and Vodafone prefer using some positive words, like *improve*, *support* and *service* to shape a positive, approachable and easy-going corporate image, and an image of prioritizing the environmental sustainability and the well-being of people; 2) CSR reports of China Mobile contain the keywords *poverty* and *alleviation*, which means China Mobile is pragmatic, collaborative and active to assume the responsibility for social events; 3) CSR reports of Vodafone contain keywords like *privacy*, *women* and *global* as well as some other countries, which shows Vodafone is enterprising, globalized and attentive to the development of women; 4) these differences might be related to the ideology and social culture of Chinese and British companies. This study may contribute to understanding the function of CSR report and offer helpful implications for broadening the research of corporate image.

Keywords: Corporate Social Responsibility reports, corporate image, discourse analysis, corpus

1. Introduction

Started in western countries, the construction of corporate image has a history of more than 100 years. As the world's second largest economy, China has deeply integrated into the international capital market, and the corporate image has played a significant part in shaping the international image to compete with the foreign companies in international market (Hu et al., 2019). With the increasingly living pace of society, corporate image is of great significance to the development of a company. A good corporate image can leave a good impression on its stakeholders, thus helping the company to build a firm relationship with its stakeholders and then gain more profits.

Corporate image refers to the overall impression formed by the corporate as an entity in the minds of the public (Mou and Wu, 2021), which is also an important part of national image, because Chinese companies shoulder the important responsibility of "going global" of Chinese culture and shaping the national image (Hao, 2021). In recent years, more and more attention has been paid by Chinese enterprises and scholars to corporate images. Whereas, most of the studies focused only on companies' profiles and news, few of them studied corporate image represented in Corporate Social Responsibility (CSR) reports.

CSR report is voluntarily released by enterprises according to their own needs, mainly displaying and publicizing the non-profit social responsibilities or obligations performed by enterprises to society and the public (Che and Li, 2021). So, from the CSR report, people can get more information and make an appraisal of the company. In this way, CSR reports gradually become one of the important ways for enterprises to shape and improve their corporate images.

In the past decade, with continuous emphasis on social responsibility from all walks of life, scholars from different disciplines have conducted multi-angle analyses of CSR reports in various industries (Hao, 2021) (like automobile, oil, or logistics). However, there is a lack of research into the telecommunications industry. In light of this, we are going to analyze two telecommunication companies, China Mobile Limited and Vodafone Group, so as to conduct a comparative analysis of Chinese and British companies' corporate image.

Based on the critical discourse analysis by Fairclough and corpus-based analysis, the present study aims to probe the linguistic features and corporate images represented in China Mobile's and Vodafone's CSR reports and explore the similarities and differences in using the vocabulary to present their corporate images. To some extent, this study is significant to stakeholders and companies. Not only can it help them to understand and take use of the information in CSR reports, it can also help domestic companies expand abroad wisely and efficiently. Analyzing the characteristics of Chinese and British CSR reports will also be helpful for writers and translators of CSR reports.

2. Literature Review

2.1 Corporate Image from the View of "Constructing by Others"

*Corresponding author: Liang Xu (ndxuliang@163.com; ndxuliang@stu.xjtu.edu.cn)

A news report on a company is one of the resources for researching its corporate image. Some research adopted the corpus-assisted discourse study as method, which avoided some subjective factors and complicated data collecting and processing procedures. Zhao (2021) worked on news about China's Anbang Insurance Group's acquisition of Starwood from China Daily and The New York Times. It showed that western news tended to present a negative image of Chinese companies, which was avaricious and threatening. Zuo (2019) chose 2009-2016 and 2017-2019 these two periods of reports on Huawei company from American mainstream media, including The New York Times, Washington Post and so on, to conduct comparative research. The findings were that, as a representative of the country's scientific and technological strength, Huawei has been boycotted by the United States, and negative reports on Huawei have also increased.

Questionnaire and interview are ways to collect appraisals from individuals, organizes, etc. The two ways can directly get the participants' evaluation of the company, but they may be subjective and complex. Streimikiene et al. (2020) conducted a questionnaire on 400 adults in the budget airline sector in Lithuania. It found that CSR in the budget airline sector was important for the Lithuanian customers. Nguyen and Leblanc (2001) interviewed consumers from three service industries: namely 222 consumers in retail services, 171 in telecommunications services and 395 in educational services to survey the relationships between corporate image, corporate reputation and customer loyalty. Compared with Streimikiene et al. (2020), the questionnaire conducted by Nguyen and Leblanc was quite representative, for its plentiful subjects and wide range of investigation. Mostafa et al. (2015), however, explored direct and indirect reasons that contribute to corporate image formation in a service recovery context. It mainly analyzed the complaints in interviews and mails from customers and revealed the importance of perceived justice in corporate image formation, which also provided a new perspective to research the corporate image.

2.2 Corporate Image from the View of "Personal Cultivation"

Apart from the research on corporate image from the point of "constructing by others", numerous researchers also devoted themselves to the "personal cultivation" of the corporate image, which refers to the company image created by an enterprise or its employees through language, pictures, or their specific behaviors.

Company profile is a means of publicity for the company, and the way a company introduces itself to the outside world (Li and Xu, 2021). Li and Xu (2021) collected company profiles of companies that were in the list of China's top 500 companies published in Fortune magazine in 2019, excluding companies without English company profiles. And the selected enterprises covered a wide range, including internet service, real estate, medicine and so on. Its range is quite wide that might ignore personalities. Therefore, this study focuses on two companies in one industry. Xu and Zi (2020) also surveyed the company profile, selecting the Chinese and British company profiles of 100 listed companies and building a Chinese-English Parallel of Corporate Introduction to investigate the hidden corporate image constructing strategies in the English translation of the corporate publicity. Its comparative corpus is beneficial to enrich the content of Chinese image research and deepen the connotation of Chinese image research.

With the development of network platforms, the main carrier of corporate communication in China has changed from traditional media to network media with a high degree of multi-modality and strong interaction (Deng and Feng, 2021). Many companies make use of network media, like WeChat posts, websites, etc. to expand their influence. In the light of the increasing network, many scholars put their eye on research on hypertexts. Deng and Feng (2021) analyzed 90 WeChat posts of Catering companies during the COVID-19 outbreak (January 25 to February 25, 2020). It indicated that these companies assume the responsibility to ensure health and safety, popularize public epidemic prevention knowledge and convey positive attitudes, shaping a corporate image of caring for the public and giving back to the society. Meanwhile, Mou and Wu (2021) focused on the hypertexts of companies. It followed the time and provided other researchers a new perspective to research the corporate image. Nevertheless, it only made suggestions to improve hypertexts of companies from the discourse features of hypertext, not analyzed the existing hypertext, which may lose the readability and credibility.

2.3 Corporate Image Represented in CSR reports

Corporate Social Responsibility report usually introduces its company's sustainable strategies, policies, management, and revenues through three aspects: economy, society, and environment to indirectly communicate with stakeholders. And in the past few decades, CSR report has attracted increasing interest of many scholars and institutions around the world. Wu and Habek (2021) noted the trends in CSR reporting practices of Chinese listed companies. Britzelmaier et al. (2012) pointed out the most important trends and aspects of CSR reporting in China, and given some suggestions to enhance the receptivity of the stakeholders and the usefulness of the CSR report. Lock and Seele (2016) also researched the credibility of CSR reports, but it is an empirical study. It analyzed 237 CSR reports from 11 European countries.

CSR report with high credibility can shape a positive and reliable corporate image. Apart from the research on credibility of the CSR report, many scholars shone lights on the language of the CSR report to analyze the implicit corporate image. Ika et al. (2021) researched CSR reports of 12 agriculture companies listed on the Indonesia Stock Exchange (IDX) by using the content analysis. Results indicated that size positively influence CSR report in the agriculture industry, which means the larger the firm, the more resources available for the firm to do CSR activities.

Xia and Xu (2020), based on systemic functional linguistics, conducted an eco-discourse analysis of CSR reports of Geely and Diamler. It mainly analyzed the unmarked themes like "WE" "Geely" or "Diamler" and the word "EMISSION" in these two companies' CSR reports. However, Hu and Sheng (2020) studied a wide range of the linguistics in CSR reports of Huawei, BT and Telstra, such as high-frequency nouns and verbs, keywords and their collocates. Similar to Hu and Sheng (2020), Hao (2021) also analyzed language in CSR reports of two logistic company, Sinotrans Limited and FedEx Corporate.

The above studies analyzed the CSR reports from discourse perspectives, promoting the progress of research related to different disciplines, and disclosing the corporate image shaped by companies in multiple industries through CSR reports. However, telecommunication industry hasn't been studied yet. Therefore, the study will analyze the characteristics of language in CSR reports of China Mobile Limited and Vodafone Group, aiming to underline the similarities and differences in two companies' images.

3. Methodology

3.1 Research Questions

We intend to answer the following three questions:

1) What corporate images are represented in CSR reports of China Mobile and Vodafone?
2) What are the similarities and differences between the corporate image of Chinese and British telecommunication companies on CSR reports?
3) What are the underlying reasons of different corporate images represented in CSR reports of China Mobile and Vodafone?

3.2 Corpus

The two companies' English version of CSR reports were downloaded from their official websites, and 10 CSR reports from 2011~2020 as data to establish two small sub-corpora of China Mobile and Vodafone respectively. Their main features are summarized in Table 1.

Corporate	Period	No. of Text	Tokens	Total Tokens
China Mobile	2011~2020	10	291,668	721,236
Vodafone	2011~2020	10	429,568	

Table 1: Corpus description

It can be seen that 721,236 tokens are in these twenty CSR reports, which is too large to be analyzed by hand, so we applied the corpus tool AntConc for data analysis. The above data were selected as following reasons: Firstly, both China Mobile and Vodafone are influential telecommunication companies around the world. In 2021, there are 16 telecommunication companies in the Fortune 500. China Mobile is a Chinese company and ranks high in the list of the Fortune 500. And Vodafone, a telecommunication company of the United Kingdom, is one of the biggest telecommunication companies in the world. Hence, selecting the two companies is conducive to studying the impact of business ability and cultural differences on corporate image under the similar capacity and different social systems. Secondly, the two sub-corpora have relatively ideal comparability. A time span of 10 years is sufficiently large for analysis. The two companies' CSR reports are all used to introduce the companies' sustainable development strategy, annual performance and policies.

3.3 Analytical Framework

Based on Fairclough's (1992) Critical Discourse Analysis (CDA) theory, this thesis aims to analyze the image of China Mobile and Vodafone on the basis of a comparative analysis of the linguistic characteristics of these two companies' CSR reports.

CDA stems from Critical Linguistics, which is an analytical method of researching discourse from the perspective of criticism (Wang and Yang, 2008). Fairclough (1992) drew together language analysis and social theory upon a combination of more social-theoretical sense of discourse with the textual and interactive sense in linguistically-oriented discourse analysis. Hence, he created a three-dimensional discourse analysis framework that includes the text dimension, concerning to language analysis of texts; the discursive practice dimension, specifying the nature of the processes of text production and interpretation; the social practice dimension, attending to issues of concern in social analysis.

In fact, as far as Hu and Sheng (2020) were concerned, discourse and social culture contain and interact with one another. On the one hand, the use of language has an impact on the reproduction or renewal of social culture, which includes ideology, that is the power of discourse. On the other hand, discourse itself constitutes social culture, because it not only describes the world, but also constructs social relations and identities. As a consequence, we tend to analyze CSR reports from the points of text, discursive practice and social practice.

3.4 Research Procedure

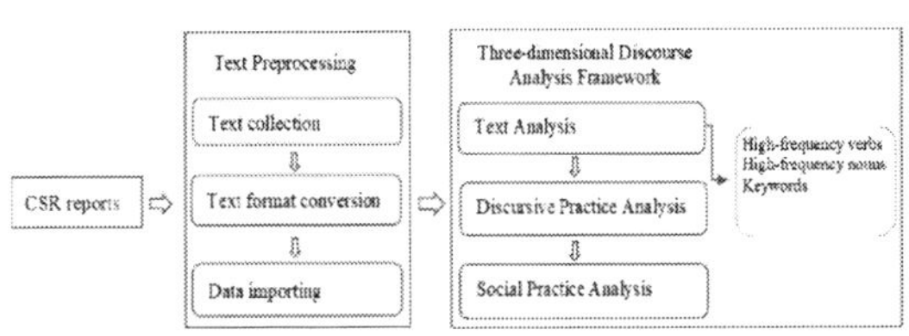

Figure 1: Research structure diagram of the study

Figure 1 above is an overview of the research procedure, and the details are described as follows.

Firstly, the PDF files of these two companies' CSR reports were collected. Secondly, those PDF files were transformed to txt format in order to be easily analyzed by AntConc. Thirdly, after text collection and text format conversion, AntConc will be employed to carry out text descriptive analysis. The specific processes are: (1) adopting "word list" in AntConc to attain the table of high-frequency nouns and verbs; (2) making a comparison between China Mobile and Vodafone through "keywords".

Then we intend to analyze the discursive practice of China Mobile and Vodafone CSR reports, explaining the processes of text production interpretation, and the relationship between the text and the discursive practice. The comparison of these two companies' image represented in CSR reports would be conducted. The relationship between the two companies' CSR reports and social culture and ideology behind the corporate image would also be explored.

4. Results and Discussion

4.1 Text Analysis of CSR Reports

Text analysis can be organized under four main headings: "vocabulary", "grammar", "cohesion", and "text structure" (Fairclough, 1992). The "vocabulary" is mainly analyzed, while other three parts will be partially included. As such, we will extract the words in CSR reports of China Mobile and Vodafone to generate two pictures of word cloud (figure 2)， which give an overview of situation of vocabulary in two companies' CSR reports. *China Mobile* and *Vodafone* are excluded, because they are normal words in these CSR reports and are not very important in this process.

Figure 2: Word cloud of China Mobile

Figure 3: Word cloud of Vodafone

The Figure 2 shows that words, like *service, employee, manage, inform, custom, company, system, develop,* are extensively used in CSR reports of China Mobile. From Figure 3, while besides those words in China Mobile, it can be seen that CSR reports of Vodafone highly used *market, report, busy, use, emission, supplier, energy, etc.* This may be related to the global strategy implemented by Vodafone. Also, from the word clouds, it shows that both China Mobile and Vodafone frequently apply content words to reveal the things that they concerned. Hence, in the next section, the content words, like verbs and nouns, are analyzed to find out the behavioral characteristics of China Mobile and Vodafone.

4.1.1 Behavioral Characteristics Presented in Content Words

Usually, high-frequency content words reflect the work or problems concerned by the speaking subject, describe the actions taken by the speaking subject, and involve what the speaking subject thinks, says and does, hence being directly applied to shape the image of the speaking subject (Hu and Sheng, 2020). In this way, the article mainly studies the verbs and nouns to find out the behavioral characteristics of China Mobile and Vodafone.

4.1.1.1 High-frequency Verbs

As Fairclough (1992) put it, the word can happen differently in different times and places and for different groups of people. Therefore, the table only picks words with higher frequency and removes other forms of the same word with lower frequency for they actually represent the same action but actions in different condition. In the meantime, to look for representative actions of two companies, the table collected the top 20 high-frequent verbs to analyze their log-likelihood ratio and significance. And the standardized frequency is calculated as the following formula:

$$\text{normalized frequency} = \frac{\text{raw frequency}}{\text{total number of tokens}} \times 10000$$

In the meantime, the same top 20 high-frequency verbs are selected out, and then the rest top 20 high-frequency verbs of China Mobile and Vodafone are compared with the corresponding words in China Mobile or Vodafone respectively. The reason for this is to analyze their log-likelihood ratio and significance. Thereupon, a word table of two corpora through AntConc is created, while the sequence of the table is in the order of log-likelihood ratios. The specific information is shown in Table 2.

As we can see from Table 2, in China Mobile CSR reports, there exist some high frequent verbs like *have, use, support, improve, help, provide, etc.*, are the same words as some high frequent verbs in Vodafone CSR reports. While among these words, the words *have, support, use, help, etc.*, have strong statistical significance($p<0.001$), and there is non-significance in words *improve*, *provide*, *waste*, *need* ($p>0.05$). Hence, by analyzing these words with non-significance, we find that they are positive words, which indicates that the two enterprises have made great efforts to present a positive image of willing to offer services and help to the public and their employees.

No.	High-frequency Verbs	China Mobile Raw Freq.	China Mobile Normalized Freq.	Vodafone Raw Freq.	Vodafone Normalized Freq.	Log-likelihood Ratio	P
1	see	62	2.13	544	12.66	275.93	0.000***
2	operate	20	0.69	284	6.61	183.04	0.000***
3	built	164	5.62	37	1.27	143.34	0.000***
4	focus	77	2.64	410	9.54	139.16	0.000***
5	include	44	1.51	304	7.08	130.56	0.000***
6	use	327	11.21	956	22.25	126.35	0.000***
7	support	619	21.22	467	10.87	120.64	0.000***
8	promote	284	9.74	141	4.83	120.26	0.000***
9	have	875	30	1984	46.19	118.78	0.000***
10	carried	153	5.25	50	1.71	102.21	0.000***
11	launched	284	9.74	164	5.62	95.68	0.000***
12	believe	25	0.86	197	4.59	93.17	0.000***
13	ensure	186	6.38	551	12.83	75.13	0.000***
14	manage	57	1.95	255	5.94	70.80	0.000***
15	enable	51	1.75	234	5.45	67.07	0.000***
16	implemented	165	5.66	89	3.05	61.98	0.000***
17	reduce	151	5.18	427	9.94	51.99	0.000***
18	developed	280	9.6	216	7.41	51.53	0.000***
19	help	275	9.43	635	14.78	40.90	0.000***
20	monitoring	199	6.82	152	5.21	37.58	0.000***
21	made	197	6.75	157	5.38	33.20	0.000***
22	continued	162	5.55	140	4.8	21.37	0.000***
23	increase	112	3.84	270	6.29	20.41	0.000***
24	related	160	5.49	318	10.9	9.85	0.002**
25	needs	178	6.1	301	7.01	2.16	0.14
26	provide	320	10.97	426	9.92	1.86	0.17
27	waste	182	6.24	276	6.43	0.09	0.76
28	improve	346	11.86	508	11.83	0.00	0.96

Table 2: High-frequency Verbs Comparison

Although China Mobile and Vodafone have some same high frequent verbs, the collocates of these verbs are different. Take the verb "improve" as an example, making "improve" as a retrieval item and putting it in the "Concordance" in AntConc, we can get some concordance lines shown in (1), and (2), which shows that *customer*, *management and network* are highly collocated with "improve" in China Mobile CSR reports, while in Vodafone CSR reports, *energy*, *people* and *efficiency* are always appeared to the right of "improve" (partial concordance lines are displayed in No. 3 to 4). Thereupon, China Mobile tends to pay attention to the process, but Vodafone takes high priority to the results.

(1) We then established company-wide benchmarks of best practice in 3 areas including problem solving, management process and support mechanism in order to **improve network** quality. (China Mobile, 2011)

(2) We conduct company-wide customer satisfaction survey, collecting over 300,000 samples nationwide each year and using the survey data to evaluate the business performance of provincial subsidiaries as well as **improve** our **customer** satisfaction. (China Mobile, 2014)

(3) The push to **improve energy efficiency** across our networks is a fantastic opportunity to cut our carbon footprint and reduce costs. (Vodafone, 2012)

(4) We will innovate to **improve** access to finance, education and healthcare; **improve efficiency** in agriculture and working; and deliver low carbon solutions. (Vodafone, 2013)

Also, different from Vodafone CSR reports, *launched*, *promote*, *developed* etc. are mostly shown in China Mobile CSR reports. These words are grouped with the subjects *we*, *Mobile or mobile,* adjuncts *internal*, *remote*, *jointly*, *actively*, etc. and objects *system(s), mechanism* (see concordance lines in No. 5 to 6). And in Vodafone CSR reports, *reduce*, *focus*, *set*, *operate* and so on present highly. They always appear with *network*, *information*, *digital*, *chains*, *global*, *energy*, *emissions*, *carbon* and so on (see some concordance lines in 7 to 8). From this, the findings are that China Mobile lays emphasis both on internal and external development, cooperation and management, while Vodafone focuses on the development of products, services and environment.

(5) **We** have **actively launched** dedicated programmes focusing on the protection of the rights of our female employees. (China Mobile, 2012)

(6) **We actively developed** information technologies and devices which can execute fire positioning and real-time monitoring and directing to enhance forest security. (China Mobile, 2011)

(7) Our Carbon Connections study established the potential for mobile to improve business efficiency and **reduce carbon emissions**, identifying opportunities that could cut carbon emissions by 113 megatonnes by 2020 in Europe alone. (Vodafone,

2011)

(8) We **operate** a **global information** governance system that enables us to track the flow of customer data and ensure we apply appropriate governance and legal processes. (Vodafone, 2013)

Therefore, the corporate image of China Mobile is pragmatic, collaborative, and positive. Vodafone's corporate image is enterprising and sustainable.

4.1.1.2 High-frequency Nouns

Compared with verbs, nouns mainly indicate the things companies concerned about. Therefore, taking the same process as previous step, some controversial words with double part of speech were excluded, such as *control*, *approach*, *work* etc., and the rest top 20 high-frequency nouns were selected because they present the central point of two companies, which can be more representative.

The same top 20 high-frequency nouns are selected out, and the rest high-frequency nouns of China Mobile and Vodafone are compared with the corresponding words in China Mobile or Vodafone. See the details on Table 3.

No.	High-frequency Nouns	China Mobile Raw Freq.	China Mobile Normalized Freq.	Vodafone Raw Freq.	Vodafone Normalized Freq.	Log-likelihood Ratio	P
1	China	2522	86.47	20	0.47	4353.67	0.000***
2	Company	962	32.98	38	0.88	1458.21	0.000***
3	markets	26	0.89	1092	25.42	931.82	0.000***
4	system	894	30.65	160	3.72	886.95	0.000***
5	Mobile	2174	74.54	1165	27.12	824.72	0.000***
6	development	967	33.15	292	6.8	689.82	0.000***
7	women	12	0.41	681	15.85	606.36	0.000***
8	poverty	456	15.63	39	0.91	593.06	0.000***
9	platform	497	17.04	106	2.47	449.05	0.000***
10	management	1308	44.85	761	17.72	435.18	0.000***
11	countries	81	2.78	670	15.6	327.34	0.000***
12	emissions	222	7.61	1050	24.44	312.31	0.000***
13	consumption	506	17.35	248	5.77	218.06	0.000***
14	people	286	9.81	996	23.19	189.14	0.000***
15	information	1118	38.33	905	21.07	180.28	0.000***
16	safety	287	9.84	974	22.67	176.41	0.000***
17	suppliers	396	13.58	1189	27.68	167.23	0.000***
18	health	214	7.34	727	16.92	131.92	0.000***
19	level	445	15.26	297	6.91	114.65	0.000***
20	network	712	24.41	619	14.41	92.08	0.000***
21	Group	384	13.17	964	22.44	83.54	0.000***
22	business	490	16.8	1142	26.58	76.24	0.000***
23	areas	451	15.46	372	8.66	68.83	0.000***
24	industry	446	15.29	382	8.89	60.57	0.000***
25	technology	286	9.81	710	16.53	59.32	0.000***
26	data	566	19.41	1077	25.07	24.94	0.000***
27	service	866	29.69	1035	24.09	20.41	0.000***
28	employees	1037	35.55	1283	29.87	17.29	0.000***
29	customers	577	19.78	1050	24.44	16.98	0.000***
30	energy	691	23.69	985	22.93	0.43	0.51
31	Vodafone	0	0	3491	81.27	###	###

Table 3: High-frequency Noun Comparison

From Table 3, we can know that *employees*, *service(s)*, *energy*, *data*, *information*, *business*, *customers* and *management* appear in these two CSR reports. Among these words, only one word *energy* in two companies' CSR reports lacks significance ($p>0.05$). Other words, like *employees*, *data*, *information*, etc., reach the statistical significance ($p<0.001$). However, though *employees*, *service(s)*, *customers*, *work*, and *data* have statistical significance, their log-likelihood ratios are quite low, which indicates that China Mobile and Vodafone tend to use these words in their CSR reports. Therefore, we can draw the conclusion that both two companies attach importance to employees, services, business and so on, which is similar to the result of the research on Huawei company's image (Hu and Sheng, 2020). This is because CSR report emphasizes a company's progress of social responsibility obtained during a year. The differences are as follows.

Though the two companies have the same high frequent nouns, *employees*, *information*, *management*, and *energy* in China Mobile CSR reports are used more frequent than the words in Vodafone, which can be seen from the normalized frequency, vice versa. Furthermore, we find that "employees" highly collocates with *encourage*, *protect*, and *help*; "information" is in line with *security*; "management" is presented with, *environmental* and *system*; and "energy" highly appears with *saving*, *conservation*, *reduce* and *consumption* (see details from No. 9 to 11). Depending on this, we can know that China Mobile pays close attention to the development of employees, information safety, and environmental sustainability.

(9) To improve career development mechanism and **encourage employees'** development; To **care for** employees' health and take various measures to **help** employees achieve work-life balance. (China Mobile, 2011)

(10) To enhance consumption transparency, protect **information security** and customer privacy and foster a healthy consumption environment; (China Mobile, 2011)

(11) we have implemented an overarching Green Action Plan which focuses on energy conservation and emissions reduction to improve our performance in **environmental management, energy** conservation and emissions reduction from the perspective of our company, supply chain and the society. (China Mobile, 2012)

As for Vodafone, the rate of *business, data, and customers* is higher than these words in China Mobile CSR reports. Through retrieving, it shows that "business" collocates with *sustainable*, *strategy*, *performance*, etc.; "data" comes with *customer*, *protection*, etc.; "customers" presents with *female*, *privacy*, *information*, etc. (see details from No. 12 to 15). The results disclose that Vodafone emphasizes on the development of the company, female rights or equality and privacy of data and customers.

(12) We aim to grow our **business** in a **sustainable** way. (Vodafone, 2012)

(13) …to the business on the rights and interests of Vodafone Germany's customers regarding privacy and **data protection**. (Vodafone, 2014)

(14) By tailoring our services for women, we aim to attract more **female customers** at the same time as bringing the benefits of better access to telecommunications to them and their families. (Vodafone, 2011)

(15) In realising this ambition, safeguarding **customers' privacy** and security, and protecting younger users from inappropriate content and contact online, is increasingly important. (Vodafone, 2011)

Also, "poverty" specially performs as high-frequent nouns in China Mobile CSR reports. Through analyzing the concordance lines that contained these nouns, the finding is that "poverty" tends to group with *alleviation*, *relief*, *reduction*, *elimination*, *stricken areas*, etc. This underscores that China Mobile prioritizes doing its part in solving the social problem. And "emissions" and "women" particularly show in Vodafone CSR reports. Also, retrieving "emissions" and "women" respectively, we can see that "emissions" collocates with *carbon*, *gas*, *reduce*, etc.; "women" is in line with *empower*, *ensure*, *enable*, *connect*, *inspire*, etc. Thus, Vodafone is responsible for the development of women and environment.

According to the analysis above, the corporate image of China Mobile is responsible for people, society and surroundings. Vodafone's corporate image is putting high value on equality, customers and privacy. Both China Mobile and Vodafone take environmental sustainability seriously.

4.1.2 Focal Features Presented in Keywords

Keywords are important words. Scott and Tribble (2006) explained keyness as quality words that may have in a given text or set of texts, demonstrating that they are important, and they reflect what the text is really about. While Scott and Bondi (2010) explained the words with keyness are prominent in some way in a text, and their prominence may lead people to perceive the aboutness of the whole text or of certain parts of it, and it may assist people to perceive something about the style of the text which is different from styles of other texts.

According to the instructions in AntConc, keywords of China Mobile's CSR reports should take Vodafone's CSR reports for reference, vice versa, then compared with Vodafone's CSR reports, words appear more frequently in China Mobile's CSR reports are keywords of the CSR reports, and relatively, the frequency of the keyword is keyness. The specific situation of this keyword list is shown in Table 4.

	China Mobile CSR		Vodafone CSR	
	Keywords	Keyness	Keywords	Keyness
1	China	4353.67	Vodafone	3617.98
2	Mobile	3842.64	markets	931.82
3	Company	1458.21	women	626.07
4	system	886.95	UK	491.00
5	Limited	748.02	working	418.27
6	Management	700.38	India	407.29
7	development	689.82	see	351.74
8	poverty	593.06	countries	327.34
9	Number	560.55	privacy	317.01
10	CSR	556.08	emissions	312.31
11	alleviation	487.08	Code	308.80
12	service	458.19	Africa	298.96
13	yuan	458.11	tax	298.24
14	Indicators	452.68	section	286.86
15	platform	449.05	global	275.56
16	management	435.18	emerging	274.48
17	provincial	425.52	country	243.18
18	communication	419.46	contractors	226.32
19	construction	415.79	example	213.90
20	Internet	413.31	Tanzania	213.49

Table 4: Keywords Comparison

Table 4 exposes that, the highest keyness of keywords are the names of the two companies, China Mobile and Vodafone, indicating that corporate image is highly respected by these two companies.

China Mobile's keywords are *China*, *Mobile*, *Company*, *alleviation*, *poverty*, *system*, *platform*, *communication*, *service*, etc. Hence, China Mobile focuses on social problems like the fight against poverty. Vodafone includes the keywords: *Vodafone*, *women*, *markets* and so on. This reveals that Vodafone assumes more responsibility of women. In particular, countries like *India*, *the UK*, *Africa*, *Tanzania* have high keyness. Thus, Vodafone focuses on its globalization strategy.

Above all, China Mobile is people foremost and responsible for social issues. And Vodafone is internationalized and pays attention to human rights.

4.2 Discursive Practice Analysis of China Mobile and Vodafone CSR Reports

As Fairclough (1992) put it, discursive practice involves processes of text production, distribution and consumption, and the nature of these steps varies between different types of discourse according to social factors. And since 2006, China Mobile has released Chinese and English version of CSR reports annually. While Vodafone published the CSR reports much earlier in 2000. The reports are prepared in accordance with the core option of the GRI (Global Reporting Initiative) standards, focusing on the information about its economic, social and environmental sustainability development.

4.2.1 Differences in Source of Information

Fairclough (1992) mentioned that texts have variable outcomes of an extra-discursive as well as a discursive sort. For example, some texts lead to war or to the destruction of nuclear weapons; others to people losing or gaining jobs; others change people's attitudes, beliefs or practices. Therefore, take the 2020 English version of China Mobile's CSR report as an instance, to increase the credibility of the CSR reports, China Mobile collected its data and information from various channels, such as the relevant internal data collection system and statistical reports of the company (The information comes from the page 62 of the 2020 China Mobile's CSR report). In the same way, take 2020 version of Vodafone's CSR report as an example, unlike China Mobile, Vodafone used an electronic collection process (The information comes from the page 29 of the 2020 Vodafone's CSR report). In addition, much data of the CSR reports is gathered through technology and suppliers, which is in accordance with the high-frequency nouns shown in the Table 3. Therefore, the applied strategies would influence the languages in CSR reports, then have an impact on the renderings of the corporate image.

4.2.2 Differences in Usage of the Cases, Pictures and Figures

In order to illustrate its work on society, economy and the environment more clearly and precisely, China Mobile wielded large numbers of cases, pictures and figures. For example, from page 4 to 11 in China Mobile's CSR report 2020, there are numerous figures, 5 cases and more than 10 pictures and graphics. This supporting information shows the concrete data in a direct way, which is easier for readers to get the information and understand the achievement that China Mobile has obtained, building an image of credible and responsible. Nevertheless, Vodafone Group applied much less cases and pictures in the 2020 report than China Mobile CSR report 2020 and its previous CSR reports like CSR report in 2014~2015. The reason may be that Vodafone breaks down the content and put the content in dedicated reports.

4.3 Social Practice Analysis of China Mobile and Vodafone CSR Reports

According to Fairclough's three-dimensional discourse analysis framework, social practice analysis under the perspective of critical discourse analysis aims to unveil the social practice factors influencing the production and interpretation of discourse or social culture factors including ideology (Hu and Sheng, 2020). Compared with Vodafone CSR reports during 2011 to 2020, China Mobile CSR reports are in the social practice of poverty eradication. Hence, the high frequent vocabularies are *poverty, alleviation and so on*. While Vodafone is under a social culture of human rights, individualism, equality as well as industrialization. Therewith, their reports have many words like *privacy*, *equality*, *women*, *technology*, etc.

5. Conclusion

Owing to the self-built corpora of China Mobile and Vodafone, and the appliance of the Fairclough's three-dimensional discourse analysis framework, this paper analyzes the corporate image represented in these two companies' CSR reports, finds out the similarities and differences among these reports, and reveals the implicit ideology factors to the differences. The findings manifest the similarities: two companies are all sustainable, positive, and human-centered. While the differences are that, as a state-owned enterprise, China Mobile pays more attention to its effort to solving the social problem, poverty; Vodafone tends to help women gain equality and has the ambition to expand its business. Additionally, through social practice analysis, the ideology and social culture have an impact on the difference between Chinese and foreign companies.

To sum up, it should be noted that this research, to some extent, develops the research of enterprises in telecommunication industry, and attributes to the external propaganda work of Chinese companies. However, some shortcomings should be pointed out: (1) the size of corpora is small, thus may lack the representativeness; (2) there already existed several studies on the vocabulary, hence future research can try to extend to the rhetoric or typical sentences.

Acknowledgments

We greatly appreciate the anonymous reviewers for their constructive and insightful comments. This study was supported by Jiangxi Provincial Social Science Foundation (No. 21YY05). At the completion of it, we would like to thank Professor Weiping Wu, Dr. Xiaorong Zeng and Dr. Zeyuan Chen for their warm encouragement to conduct the present study and insightful suggestions in revising the manuscript.

Bibliographical References

Britzelmaier B, Kraus P, and Xu Y. (2012). An overview of CSR reporting development in China. *World Review of Entrepreneurship Management & Sustainable Development*, 8(3): 319-339.

Che Siqi, and Li Xuepei. (2021). A Comparative Study of the Discourse on Emotions of Chinese and American CEO's Letters from the Perspective of Appraisal System-Text Mining Based on Sentiment Dictionary and Machine Learning. *Journal of Foreign Languages (Journal of Shanghai*

International Studies University), 44(02):50-59.
Deng Yi, and Feng Dezheng. (2021). Multimodal Discourse Construction of Corporate Social Responsibility in Public Health Crisis. *Foreign Language Education,* 42(5):13-18.
Fairclough, N. (1992). Discourse and Social Change. *Cambridge: Polity Press*.
Hao Jialiang. (2021). A Corpus-based Study on Corporate Social Responsibility Reports and Corporate Image. *Journal of Weinan Normal University,* 36(08):51-59.
Hu Kaibao, and Sheng Dandan. (2020). The Image of Huawei Corporation in the English Translations of *Sustainable Development Report*. *Journal of Foreign Languages (Journal of Shanghai International Studies University)*, 43(06): 94-106.
Hu Yu, Wang Shuaidong, and Wang Jiajing. (2019). On Corporate Image. *Beijing: CITIC Publishing House.*
Ika S R, Akbar FA, Puspitasari D, Sumbodo B T, et al. (2021). Corporate social responsibility reporting of agriculture companies: evidence from Indonesia. *IOP Conference Series: Earth and Environmental Science*, 800(1).
Lock I, and Seele P. (2016). The credibility of CSR (corporate social responsibility) reports in Europe. Evidence from a quantitative content analysis in 11 countries. *Journal of Cleaner Production*, 122 (may 20): 186-200.
Li Yi, and Xu Xueping. (2021). The Discursive Construction of Chinese Enterprises' institutional Identity under the Background of Overseas Market. *Foreign Languages and Literatures,* 38(3):13.
Mostafa R B, Lages C R, Shabbir H A, et al. (2015). Corporate image: a service recovery perspective. *Journal of Service Research*, 18(4): 468-483.
Mou Yiwu, and Wu Yun. (2021). Study on Enhancing China's Corporate Image by Hypertext Translation. *Computer-assisted Foreign Language Education,* (03):115-120+18.
Nguyen N, and Leblanc G. (2001). Corporate image and corporate reputation in customers' retention decisions in services. *Journal of Retailing & Consumer Services*, 8(4): 227-236.
Scott M, and C Tribble. (2006). Textual Patterns: Key Words and Corpus Analysis in Language Education. *Amsterdam / Philadelphia: John Benjamins Publishing Company*.
Scott M, and Bondi M. (2010). Keyness in Texts.
Streimikiene D, Lasickaite K, Skare M, et al. (2020). The impact of Corporate Social Responsibility on Corporate Image: Evidence of budget airlines in Europe. *Corporate Social Responsibility and Environmental Management*.
Wang Zexia, and Yang Zhong. (2008). Interpretation and Reflection on the Three-dimensional Model of Fairclough's Discourse. *Foreign Languages Research,* (3): 9-13.
Wu Xiaojuan, and Hąbek Patrycja. (2021). Trends in Corporate Social Responsibility Reporting. The Case of Chinese Listed Companies. *Sustainability*, 13(15).
Xia Rong, Xu Jun. (2020). An Eco-Discourse Analysis of Corporate Social Responsibility: A Systemic Functional Linguistics Perspective. *Foreign Languages in China,* 17(4):33-42.
Xu Jun, and Zi Zhengquan. (2020). A Corpus-based Study on Corporate International Publicity Translation and Semantic Construction of Corporate Image. *Foreign Language Research,* (01): 93-101.
Zhao Yonggang. (2021). A Contrastive Study of Chinese Corporate Images Constructed in Media M&A Discourse: A Corpus- assisted Discourse-historical Analysis. *Journal of PLA University of Foreign Languages,* 44(01):62-70.
Zuo Mingyao. (2019). Study on Huawei's Corporate Image Transformation in reports of American Media. *Modern Marketing (Management Edition)* (08): 78-81.

Proceedings of CSR-NLP I @LREC 2022, pages 24–34
Marseille, 25 June 2022

Framing Legitimacy in CSR: A Corpus of Chinese and American Petroleum Company CSR Reports and Preliminary Analysis

Jieyu Chen[1], Kathleen Ahrens[1], Chu-Ren Huang[2]
1. Department of English and Communication, The Hong Kong Polytechnic University, Hung Hom, Kowloon, Hong Kong
2. Department of Chinese and Bilingual Studies, The Hong Kong Polytechnic University, Hung Hom, Kowloon, Hong Kong

Abstract

We examine how Chinese and American oil companies use the gain- and loss-framed BUILDING source domain to legitimize their business in Corporate Social Responsibility (CSR) reports. Gain and loss frames can create legitimacy because they can ethically position an issue. We will focus on oil companies in China and the U.S. because different socio-cultural contexts in these two countries can potentially lead to different legitimation strategies in CSR reports, which can shed light on differences in Chinese and American CSR. All of the oil companies in our data are on the Fortune 500 list (2020). The results showed that Chinese oil companies used BUILDING metaphors more frequently than American oil companies. The most frequent keyword in Chinese CSRs "build" highlights environmental achievements in compliance with governments' policies. American CSRs often used the metaphorical verb "support" to show their alignment with environmental policies and the interests of different stakeholders. The BUILDING source domain was used more often as gain frames in both Chinese and American CSR reports to show how oil companies create benefits for different stakeholders.

Keywords: source domain, legitimacy, Corporate Social Responsibility

1 Introduction

The concept of organizational legitimacy is defined as "a generalized perception or assumption that the actions of an entity are desirable, proper or appropriate within some socially constructed system of norms, values, beliefs, and definitions" (Suchman, 1995, p.275). The carbon-intensive sector, particularly the petroleum industry, has a potential legitimacy gap because its business contributes to environmental impacts. This gap might motivate petroleum companies to use a range of legitimation strategies.

Of all types of corporate discourses, Corporate Social Responsibility (CSR) reports serve as an intriguing discourse for exploring how corporations legitimize their environmental performance. Due to more discretion in terms of content and template, CSR reports can exploit various means to construct reality. Therefore, CSR reports can provide more clues regarding how companies legitimize their business operations compared to other corporate documents. This study examines how legitimation strategies are used in the environmental sections of Corporate Social Responsibility (CSR) reports produced by petroleum companies to justify their environmental practice.

1.1 The Source Domain of BUILDING as a Legitimation Strategy

Previous studies on the source domain of BUILDING focus primarily on its usage in political discourse (Ahrens et al., 2021; Charteris-Black, 2004, 2016; Lu and Ahrens, 2008). Until now, few previous studies have investigated how the source domain of BUILDING is employed in business discourse. As the usage of the source domain of BUILDING in business discourse may differ from its usage in political discourse, this study aims to explore how this domain is used as a legitimation strategy to justify the environmental practice of petroleum companies in CSR reports.

Source domains can be useful in creating legitimacy because they have been found to be effective in persuasion (Charteris-Black, 2005; Chilton and Ilyin, 1993; Goatly, 2007; Kövecses, 2010; Thornborrow, 1993; Van Teeffelen, 1994). Charteris-Black (2011) argued that source domains could be used to create legitimacy by transferring "positive or negative associations of various source words to a metaphor target" (p.13). The source domain of BUILDING can be used for a legitimation purpose because it creates a sense of unity towards a socially-valued goal (Atanasova and Koteyko, 2017b; Charteris-Black, 2004, 2016). In addition, this source domain tends to construct an objective as a long-term goal, requiring patience against expectations of instant achievements (Charteris-Black, 2004, 2016). The source domain of BUILDING can also be employed flexibly in promoting various world views. Ahrens et al. (2021) observed that the BUILDING source domain was used by the British Governors and the HKSAR Chief Executives differently in terms of their relevant time frames, topics, and references, showing the source domain's utility in representing different world views.

1.2 The Source Domain of BUILDING Used as Gain and Loss Frames in CSR Reports

A variety of previous studies have investigated how source domains are used to frame climate change in different types of discourse (e.g., Atanasova and Koteyko, 2017a, 2017b; Romaine, 1996; Shaw and Nerlich, 2015). However, little research has been conducted to explore how source domains can be used as gain and loss frames.

Gain and loss frames can create legitimacy because they can ethically position an issue. The concepts of gain and loss frames come from the Prospect Theory (Tversky and Kahneman, 1981), which argues that people are biased toward risks. An alternative action framed as regards its related costs (loss frame) or benefits (gain frame) will impact people's perceptions of risks in a different manner (Tversky and Kahneman, 1981). As the environmental efforts of petroleum companies are related to environmental risks, gain and loss frames should be useful to legitimize these efforts. It would be interesting to observe how the source domain of BUILDING is used as gain and loss frames because Charteris-Black (2016) indicated that the BUILDING source domain tends to be positively connotated. It would be intriguing to see if this feature is reflected in its usages as gain and loss frames.

The gain and loss frames in CSR reports differ slightly from those in previous studies because CSR reports are read by different types of stakeholders who care for different types of interests. Bhatia (2012) categorized stakeholders into the following four major groups: "1) organizational stakeholders (such as employees, customers, shareholders, and suppliers); 2) community stakeholders (such as local residents and special interests groups); 3) regulatory stakeholders (such as municipalities, regulatory systems); 4) media stakeholders" (p. 222). For organizational stakeholders, their primary interests focus on maximizing corporate interests. For community stakeholders, regulatory stakeholders, and media stakeholders, their primary interests tend to be the pursuit of social and environmental interests. These two different interests have the potential to motivate different perceptions of risks.

1.3 Petroleum Companies in China and the U.S.

Our study compares legitimation strategies used by Chinese and American petroleum companies. China and the US are the two largest consumers of petroleum (Daojiong, 2006). The petroleum companies in these two countries are major contributors to global greenhouse gases.

Different socio-cultural contexts in China and the U.S. can motivate differences in legitimation strategies in CSR reports. China has become the world's largest net importer of petroleum since 2013 (U.S. Energy Information Administration, 2018). Apart from that, worsening air quality has motivated the Chinese government to shift from dependency on coal and oil (Ji et al., 2018). The energy gap in the U.S. is not as wide as in China. In 2019, total U.S. energy exports exceeded total energy imports (U.S. Energy Information Administration, 2020). Regarding social contexts, most major Chinese oil companies are state-owned, whereas most American oil companies are publicly owned. These different socio-cultural factors can result in differences in legitimation strategies. Differences in legitimation strategies used in Chinese and American CSR reports can shed light on differences in Corporate Social Responsibilities in China and the U.S. because legitimacy is associated with value systems, and CSR are values related to corporate activities. In this study, we will address the following research questions:

RQ1: What keywords are used in the source domains of the BUILDING in Chinese and American CSR reports and their frequencies of occurrences?

RQ2: Are there different preferences in gain and loss frames in Chinese and American CSR reports?

RQ3: Are gain/loss frames motivated more often by corporate interests or environmental interests in Chinese and American CSR reports?

2 Corpus

Our study focuses on CSR reports published by American and Chinese petroleum companies on Fortune 500 (2020) because these petroleum companies are key players in the petroleum industries by revenue in their respective countries. Stakeholders expect higher accountability and transparency in their CSR reports. In light of this, these companies will be cautious about the way they discursively construct the environmental issues in their CSR reports. Attitudes demonstrated in their CSR reports should be a relatively accurate reflection of their attitudes on social issues.

The Chinese corpus in our study has a word count of 121,751, and the American corpus is almost double the Chinese corpus, with a word count of 266,826. The corpora sizes in our study are demonstrated in Table 1:

ACSRs	CCSRs
American Petroleum Companies	**Chinese Petroleum Companies**
ExxonMobil 2010-2019 (70,789 words)	Sinopec 2010-2019 (35,387 words)
Chevron 2010-2019 (14,122 words)	China National Petroleum 2013-2019 (28,384 words)
Marathon Petroleum 2011-2019 (34,809 words)	China National Offshore Petroleum 2011,2013,2014, 2015, 2016,2017, 2018, 2019 (35,010 words)
Phillips 66 2016-2019 (6,871 words)	Sinochem 2010,2011,2012, 2013, 2014,2015, 2017,2018, 2019 (22,970 words)
Valero Energy 2015-2019 (16,801 words)	
ConocoPhillips 2011-2019 (123,434 words)	
Total 266,826	**Total 121,751**

Table 1. CSR Reports of American and Chinese Petroleum Companies

As shown in Table 1, the corpus consists of two subcorpora for comparative purposes: the American CSR reports subcorpus (henceforth, ACSRs) and the Chinese CSR report subcorpus (henceforth, CCSRs).

3 Source Domain Analysis

This study aims to explore how the BUILDING source domain is used as gain and loss frames to legitimize the environmental practice of petroleum companies in CSR reports. Our source domain analysis consists of six steps: 1) determining potential keywords; 2) source domain verification; 3) Part of Speech (POS) tagging; 4) metaphor identification; 5) identifying gain and loss frames; and 6) identifying the corporate and environmental interests behind gain and loss frames.

The first step of our source domain analysis is to determine potential keywords. Considering the large size of our corpora, we identified potential source domain keywords using Sardinha's (2012) sampling technique. In total, we collected 49 potential keywords for the source domain of BUILDING.

As for the source domain verification, we adopted the method proposed by Ahrens and Jiang (2020), which is a comprehensive approach that can be used for a variety of source domains by adding an online dictionary as well as making use of collocation patterns (Chung and Huang, 2010; Gong et al., 2008). As for the online English dictionary, we chose *Macmillan English Dictionary for Advanced Learners* (Rundell, 2002) because this dictionary is one of three dictionaries used by MIPVU (Steen et al., 2010), the metaphor identification procedure we adopt in this study.

Since the MIPVU procedure does not cross word-class boundaries when determining the metaphoricality of lexical units, we parsed our data with Part of Speech (POS) tags before the metaphor identification. The computer tool used for POS tagging is the *POS tagging* (Toutanova, et al., 2003) of *Stanford CoreNLP* (Manning et al., 2014). After determining the word classes of the source domain keywords in our study, we will then use MIPVU (Steen et al., 2010) to investigate if a keyword is used metaphorically or not. MIVPU identifies a word as a metaphor if its usage in the text shows a cross-domain mapping from its basic meaning to its contextual meaning (Steen et al., 2010). In other words, if a word's meaning in the dictionary is more basic than its meaning in the context, it is identified as a metaphor. 10% of our data (n=187) were used for the inter-rater reliability test. The result indicates the Kappa value is 0.8145, showing a strong agreement.

Previous studies suggest that the gain-framed appeal focuses on the benefits of adopting a particular action, while the loss-framed appeal emphasizes the losses of alternative action (e.g., Cho and Boster, 2008; Gallagher and Updegraff, 2012; Rothman et al., 2006; Rothman and Salovey, 1997). The criteria for identifying gain and loss frames in our study are to decide if the goal of a sentence is perceived as gaining benefits or avoiding losses. The criteria are demonstrated as follows:

a. If the goal of a sentence is perceived as gaining benefits, it is a gain frame.

b. If the goal of the sentence is perceived as avoiding losses, it is a loss frame.

c. If the goal is perceived as neither gaining benefits or avoiding losses, it is neither the gain nor loss frame.

After identifying all the gain and loss frames, we then determine if the identified gain and loss frames were motivated by corporate interests and/or environmental interests. The criteria for identifying corporate interests and environmental interests are as follows:

a. If the goal of the frame is perceived as creating corporate benefits, such as generating more profits, creating a safe workplace, improving product quality, or enhancing corporate influence, then the frame is motivated by corporate interests.

b. If the goal of the frame is perceived as creating environmental benefits, such as improving environmental conditions or preventing environmental impacts, then the frame is motivated by environmental interests.

c. If the goal of the frame is perceived as creating both corporate benefits as well as environmental benefits, then the frame is motivated by a mix of corporate interests and environmental interests.

d. If the goal of the frame is perceived as creating neither corporate benefits nor environmental benefits, then the frame is motivated by neither corporate interests nor environmental interests.

When all the above metaphor analysis procedures had been finished, we then started to investigate our data to see how BUILDING metaphors are used as gain and loss frames to legitimize the environmental practice of American and Chinese petroleum companies.

4 Gain- and Loss-framed BUILDING Source Domain

4.1 The Source Domain of BUILDING as a Legitimation Strategy

The first research question to be answered in this study is: "What keywords are used in the source domain of BUILDING in Chinese and American CSR reports and their frequencies of occurrences?" We calculated the normalized ratios (NR) per 10,000 words of the frequencies of BUILDING metaphors used in ACSRs and CCSRs. Comparing frequencies can let us know whether CCSRs and ACSRs have a preference for the source domain of BUILDING. The normalized ratios are displayed in Figure 1.

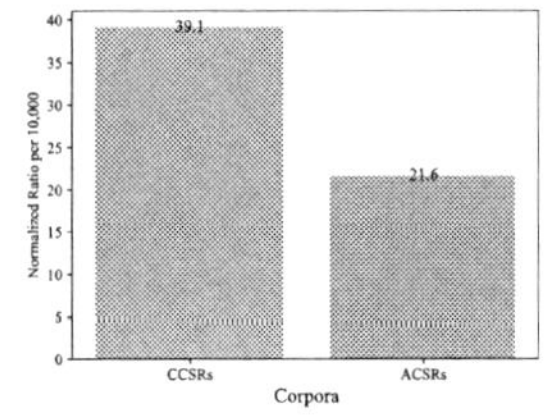

Figure 1. Normalized Rations of BUILDING Keywords in ACSRs and CCSRs

Figure 1 shows that BUILDING metaphors occur much more frequently in CCSRs than in ACSRs. A log-likelihood (LL) test was run to determine if the differences in frequencies of BUILDING metaphors are significant, with the significance level set at 0.05. The log-likelihood calculation indicates that the BUILDING source domain is significantly overused in CCSRs compared to those in ACSR (LL= +88.53), which indicates a significant difference in frequencies of BUILDING metaphors between the two corpora.

The investigation of the metaphorical expressions of the BUILDING source domain can provide a deeper insight into the characteristics of BUILDING metaphors used in CCSRs and ACSRs. These expressions are presented in three categories: "Functions," "Qualities," and "Entities." All of these expressions are demonstrated in Appendix A.

Table 1 in Appendix A shows that the BUILDING metaphor with the highest frequency is from the category of "Functions" in both corpora, which indicates that CCSRs and ACSRs tend to make use of the source domain of BUILDING to emphasize the function of a building process. The BUILDING metaphor with the highest frequency in CCSRs is "build," and the BUILDING metaphor with the highest frequency in ACSRs is "support."

The metaphor "build" can be used to present the agent of the building process as an architect who takes charge of the whole process. In many cases, the petroleum company is the architect of the building process. When discussing building a green enterprise or society, the statement is often future-oriented, which accounts for most of the usages of the metaphor "build" (n=87). The metaphor "build" is used in the past tense only when describing a specific corporate operation, which accounts for only a small portion of its usage (n=16). Examples (1) and (2) demonstrate how the metaphor "build" is used in CCSRs:

Example Sentence	Source
(1) We eliminate hidden perils from the root, enhance the safety education on all staff, strengthen energy conservation and emission reduction, disseminate the green philosophy, and promote the safe and green development, so as to make contribution to building a beautiful China.	**CCSRs** Sinochem CSR rep., 2014
(2) We participated in carbon emission trading, built a trading team, upgraded carbon assets management, and optimized carbon trading strategies, facilitating environment protection and resource conservation.	**CCSRs** Sinopec CSR rep., 2016

Table 2. Examples (1) and (2) from CCSRs

The BUILDING metaphor in Example (1) may be motivated by the conceptual metaphor SOCIETY IS A BUILDING formulated in the work of Charteris-Black (2004). Through this conceptual metaphor, *Sinochem* is presented as an active participant in China's collective efforts to construct "a beautiful China," a concept proposed in the 18th Chinese People's Congress with an aim to incorporate the construction of ecological civilization into economic, political, cultural and social constructions. As an SOE, aligning its corporate goal with a national goal helps it achieve legitimacy. As "building a beautiful China" is an ambitious goal that might require high costs, it is constructed as a future goal, with the completion date of the construction unspecified. The burdens on *Sinochem* to achieve this goal can thus be lessened.

In Example (2), however, the metaphor "build" is used in the past tense. In this sentence, the metaphor refers to a specific corporate business operation: building a team of carbon emission trading. This operation is a market-oriented approach to coping with climate change, which does not require a radical transformation of the current business model of the petroleum company and thus is favourable for organizational stakeholders. In Example (2), building a trading team is part of *Sinopec*'s efforts to develop the carbon market. Developing the carbon trading market is one of China's principal ways to achieve the dual national goal of carbon peak and carbon neutrality (Xue, 2022). The regional pilots of the carbon market system started in 2013, which finally led to the debut of the long-awaited national carbon emission trading scheme (ETS) in 2021, featuring the largest carbon market in the world by volume (Reuters, 2021). As Chinese governments show proactive support for carbon market mechanisms, the legitimacy of *Sinopec* can be realized according to China's CSR.

The BUILDING metaphor that occurs with the highest frequency in ACSRs is the verb "support."This metaphor presents the petroleum company as the lower structure of a building, which is essential for the stability of the upper part of a building. Examples (3) and (4) demonstrated the usages of the verb form of the metaphor "support" in ACSRs:

Example Sentence	Source
(3) We support the Paris Agreement as a step forward and encourage practical actions that deliver tangible results in answering the world's demands, including more energy and a cleaner environment.	**ACSRs** Chevron CSR rep., 2019
(4) In that context, Statpetroleum works with governments, businesses and other stakeholders to support viable worldwide policies and regulatory frameworks encouraging carbon-efficient solutions and the development of low-carbon technology.	**ACSRs** Conoco-Phillips CSR rep., 2011

Table 3. Examples (3) and (4) from ACSRs

In the above examples, petroleum companies used the metaphor "support" to show their compliance with environmental policies and principles. Previous studies suggest that one fundamental way to establish legitimacy is to demonstrate the congruence between the actions of an institution and social values (Richardson and Dowling, 1986; Suchman, 1995). The metaphor "support" in Example (3) aims to achieve legitimacy by manifesting the petroleum company's alignment with socially valued environmental rules and policies. In Example (3), *Chevron* indicates its support for the Paris Agreement. This message is useful for addressing concerns from regulatory, media and community stakeholders as petroleum companies have been under pressure to align their business with the Paris target.

Nevertheless, this supportive attitude is presented in parallel with the need to answer "the world's demands," with "more energy" being one of the demands. Unlike Chinese oil companies, which focus on domestic energy needs, American oil companies emphasize the world's energy demand when promoting energy development. This difference could be attributable to the fact that the U.S. has been growing into a petroleum exporter and global energy supplier in the past decade. The juxtaposition of a climate goal with an energy goal downplays the urgency of dealing with climate change and thus accommodates concerns from organizational stakeholders. In addition, the support could be just modest or symbolic as no information is provided as regards concrete supportive actions.

In Example (4), the environmental policies and rules supported by the petroleum company are to realize carbon efficiency and adopt low-carbon technology, which aligns with the interests of regulatory, media, and community stakeholders. In addition, the petroleum company indicates that the supporting power also comes from governments, businesses, and other stakeholders, which transfers part of the responsibility of coping with climate change to other stakeholders and social groups. In this way, concerns of organizational stakeholders about potential costs are accommodated. By uniting other stakeholders and the oil industry under a collective goal, the oil industry forms an alliance with stakeholders and fights side-by-side with them in the war against climate change. Potential conflicts between the oil company and its stakeholders are reconciled, and their relationship becomes collaborative.

4.2 Gain and Loss Frames

In order to answer the second research question, an exploration of whether there are different preferences in gain and loss frames in Chinese and American CSR reports is required. To this end, we identified all the gain and loss frames in both ACSRs and CCSRs, which yielded 340 gain frames and 197 loss frames in the ACSRs, and 355 gain frames and 209 loss frames in CCSRs. The frequencies of these two frames are shown in Figure 2:

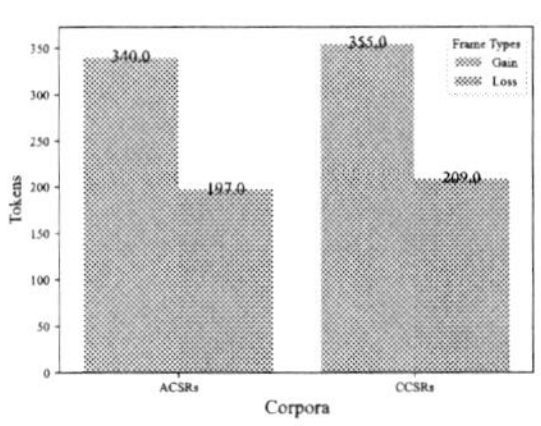

Figure 2. Gain and Loss Frames in ACSRs and CCSRs

Figure 2 shows that both ACSRs and CCSRs have a preference for gain frames. We used the goodness of fit test to confirm this observation statistically to calculate the differences between gain and loss frames in two corpora separately.

The result indicates that the CCSRs prefer to use gain frames than loss frames (X-squared = 37.794, df = 1, p-value = 7.861e-10). The calculation of goodness of fit for usages of gain and loss frames in ACSR also shows that the gain frames are used more frequently (X-squared = 38.08, df = 1, p-value = 6.79e-10). The statistical calculations of the differences between gain and loss frames in the two corpora confirmed that both ACSRs and CCSRs have a significant preference for gain frames. Nevertheless, the calculation of the effect size "Phi effect (Φ)" shows that the effect sizes are at the medium level for both statistical differences (0.2589 for CCSRs and 0.2663 for ACSRs).

The presence of loss frames in both corpora could be motivated by corporate intentions to demonstrate their transparency to achieve effective CSR communication, which requires reporting both good and bad aspects of CSR activities. Kim and Ferguson (2016, 2014) identified transparency as one of the six important communication factors expected by consumers for CSR communication. The preference for gain frames in both corpora may be attributable to the evaluative meaning of the BUILDING source domain. Charteris-Black (2004, 2016) asserted that the BUILDING source domain is positively connotated and often used to construct a socially-valued purpose or process. Therefore, ACSRs and CCSRs could use the BUILDING source domain as gain frames to conceptualize benefits generated via the achievement of a socially-valued goal. Examples (5) and (6) demonstrate how the BUILDING source domain is used as gain frames in CCSRs and ACSRs:

Sentence Examples	Source
(5) In 2018, we completed the development and industrial transformation of the independently IPR alkylate petroleum production technology, providing technical support for the production of gasoline and diesel that meet the National VI emission standards.	**CCSRs** Sinopec CSR rep., 2018
(6) We recognize that the scale and growth of unconventional resource development continues to prompt significant questions among stakeholders ... We will continue to take a leadership role in working collaboratively with communities, regulators, and industry associations to manage operational risk and address questions and concerns. ExxonMobil recognizes the importance of responsible operations in maintaining stakeholder support for this significant resource.	**ACSRs** Exxon-Mobil CSR rep., 2011

Table 4. Example (5) from CCSRs and Example (6) from ACSRs

In Example (5), the adjective "technical" is used as a premodifier of the metaphor "support," emphasizing the importance of technology for realizing an environmental goal. The technology mentioned in this example is the "petroleum production technology," favourable for organizational stakeholders as petroleum is the core product of oil companies. Developing energy is a way to alleviate the domestic demand for energy in China and thus is legitimate according to China's CSR. Since this technology enables the production of gasoline and diesel to "meet the National VI emission standards," this technical support also accommodates environmental interests.

In Example (6), the legitimacy of *ExxonMobil* faces threats as the development of unconventional resources "raises significant questions" among stakeholders. *ExxonMobil* demonstrates its responsiveness to the interests of stakeholders by acknowledging the significance of their support. The legitimacy obtained by a corporation's responsiveness to constituents' interests is a typical type of pragmatic legitimacy for institutions (Suchman, 1995). The expression "maintaining" indicates that stakeholders have already given support for the unconventional resource, and *ExxonMobil* just needs to maintain this support. Given this, the challenge of handling the legitimacy gap is downplayed. Being publicly owned, American oil companies tend to pay closer attention to maintaining support from different stakeholders.

4.3 Gain and Loss Frames Motivated by Different Interests

Gain and loss frames in CSR reports are motivated by different types of interests, given the various stakeholders as the potential readership of these reports. The examination of different interests can demonstrate how potential conflicts between different interests are handled in CSR reports. We examined the different motivations of gain and loss frames by answering the third research question, "Are gain/loss frames motivated more often by corporate interests or environmental interests in Chinese and American CSR reports?" Figure 3 displays the motivations of gain and loss frames in ACSRs and CCSRs.

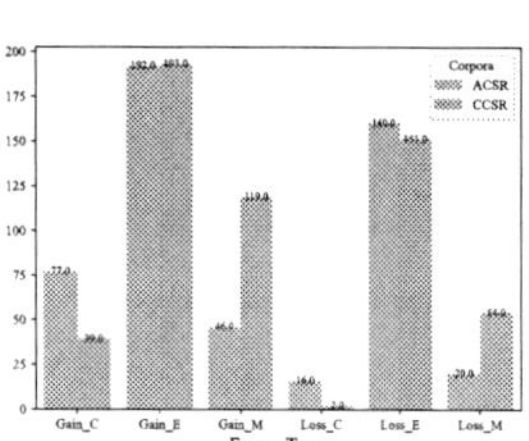

Figure 3. Gain and Loss Frames Motivated by Different Interests

Figure 3 shows that both gain and loss frames in CCSRs and ACSRs are motivated mostly by environmental interests. The above analysis results indicate that both ACSRs and CCSRs attend primarily to environmental interests. This observation is also confirmed by statistical test results (gain frames in ACSRs : X-squared = 112.7, df = 2, p-value < 2.2e-16, loss frames in ACSRs : X-squared = 205.88, df = 2, p-value < 2.2e-16, gain frames in CCSRs : X-squared = 101.4, df = 2, p-value < 2.2e-16, loss frames in CCSRs : X-squared = 165.77, df = 2, p-value < 2.2e-16). One of the reasons is that ACSRs and CCSRs are extracted from the environmental sections of CSR reports with a primary focus on environmental issues. The other reason could be that environmental interests are the primary way to achieve legitimacy as American and Chinese petroleum companies are under constant pressure in this regard.

The exploration of topics associated with different interests may indicate how petroleum companies reconcile the various interests of different stakeholders. In order to find out these topics, we extracted all the expressions that described environmental interests, corporate interests, and mixed interests in CCSRs and entered them into three plain texts "Environmental Interests CCSRs," "Corporate Interests CCSRs," and "Mixed Interests CCSRs." We uploaded all these files onto *Wmatrix* and generated the "Semantic frequent list" to obtain frequent domains associated with corporate, mixed, and environmental interests in both ACSRs and CCSRs. Only semantic domains that take up around 15% of the whole dataset are listed as top semantic domains, which are shown in Table 5.

ACSRs			CCSRs		
Environ-ment	**Corpo-rate**	**Mixed**	**Environ-ment**	**Corpo-rate**	**Mixed**
Support and Help (98)	Support and Help (33)	Leader-ship and Manage-ment (25)	Environ-ment (134)	Busi-ness: General-ly (12)	Leader-ship and Manage-ment (134)
Change (96)	Busi-ness General-ly (15)	Change (21)	Building (120)	Stability (10)	Safety (64)
Environ-ment (81)	Money and Stake-holders (14)	Science and technolo-gy (20)	Change (100)	Structur e(11)	Emergen-cy (64)
Reducti on (54)	Improve-ment (12)	Support and Help (19)	Leadersh ip and Manage-ment (86)	Improve-ment (11)	System and Frame-work (59)
Emissio n (49)	Change (12)	Risks (18)	Energy (73)	Gas (11)	Improve-ment (56)
Location s (48)	Commui-ty (10)				
426 (Freq.)	**96 (Freq.)**	**103 (Freq.)**	**513 (Freq.)**	**55 (Freq.)**	**377 (Freq.)**
3474 (Total)	**868 (Total)**	**713 (Total)**	**4083 (Total)**	**431 (Total)**	**2620 (Total)**
12% (Pct.)	**11% (Pct.)**	**14% (Pct.)**	**13% (Pct.)**	**13% (Pct.)**	**14% (Pct.)**

Table 5. Top Semantic Domains in Semantic Frequency Lists for Different Motivations in ACSRs and CCSRs

Table 5 shows that, in CCSRs, the topic "Leadership and Management" is often associated with environmental interests, as well as mixed interests. In this topic, the most frequent keyword is "management," which indicates that corporate management is essential for generating both environmental and mixed interests. The concordances of the keyword "management" indicate that CCSRs often present "management" as a building structure. One important building structure used to conceptualize corporate management is "platform." Examples (7) illustrated how the metaphor "platform" is used to conceptualize management in CCSR:

Sentence Examples	Source
(7) In order to take full advantage of information technology, CNOOC Limited began to build an environmental protection management information platform in 2011 to store all project-related data.	**CCSRs** CNOOC CSR rep., 2016

Table 6. Example (7) from CCSRs

In Example (7), the environmental protection management information is conceptualized as a platform to generate environmental interests. In CCSRs, the metaphorical usage of this keyword is often employed in reference to different abstract platforms, including technical platforms, information platforms, management platforms, learning platforms, and cooperative platforms, etc. By using this BUILDING metaphor "platform," petroleum companies present an abstract area for taking environmental activities as a tangible property of the petroleum company and the whole society. For years, China has been developing domestic Information Technology (IT) as an effective management approach. China's supportive government incentives led to the boom of domestic IT firms. Information platform has been established in almost every domestic sector in China, such as chemistry, investment, education, service, etc. Hence, building an information platform is regarded as a legitimate way to manage environmental issues according to China's CSR.

In ACSRs, the topic "Support and Help" is frequently associated with three types of interests. In this topic, the BUILDING metaphor "support" is frequently used. Example (8) demonstrates how the metaphor "support" is used in the topic "Support and Help."

Sentence Examples	Source
(8) We support well-formulated federal regulation of methane emissions from petroleum and gas exploration and production if that regulation: •Encourages early adopters and voluntary efforts. •Incorporates cost-effective innovations in technology. •Supports appropriate state-level regulations.	**ACSRs** Conoco-Phillips CSR rep., 2019

Table 7. Example (8) from ACSRs

The frequent association of the topic "Support and Help" with different interests in ACSRs indicates that different interests of stakeholders can be met with useful assistance or supportive attitudes. The metaphor "support" is used twice in Example (8). *ConocoPhillips* used the first metaphor, "support," to emphasize its supportive attitude towards regulations regarding GHG emission reductions, which helps obtain support from regulatory stakeholders. Nevertheless, this support comes with conditions: the regulations have to be "well-formulated" and "appropriate." The absence of the criteria for being "well-formulated" and "appropriate" allows the oil company to withdraw support at any time when it considers the regulations inappropriate or ill-formulated. In this vein, it would be easier for *ConocoPhillips* to reconcile corporate and environmental interests.

5 Conclusions

In this study, we explored 1) usages of keywords in the source domain of BUILDING in ACSRs and CCSRs, 2) frequencies in gain and loss frames in ACSRs and CCSRs, and 3) motivations for gain and loss frames in ACSRs and CCSRs. The topics frequently associated with various interest types were also studied. By addressing all of these issues, we have identified the following legitimation strategies of petroleum companies in Chinese and American CSR reports as well as differences in CSR in China and the U.S.

The first legitimation strategy is to use the source domain of BUILDING in different time frames so that the construction of an environmental enterprise or society is presented as a staged process. The finding of the first research question indicated that the most frequent building keyword in CCSRs was the verb "build." This BUILDING metaphor was often used by CCSRs to construct a petroleum company as an architect to create environmental achievements in compliance with government policies, such as "beautiful China" and the carbon market. The metaphor "build" was employed in the past tense to show that a specific construction stage has been completed, such as building a trading team for carbon emission trading. When the metaphor was used to conceptualize an ambitious goal, such as creating a green enterprise or society, the statement was often future-oriented. In this way, the completion of the ambitious construction was framed as a distant goal. As completion in a specific building stage has been realized, completing the ambitious construction was achievable.

The second legitimation strategy is to demonstrate the compliance of corporate activities with social norms. ACSRs often used the metaphorical verb "support" to show the petroleum company's alignment with socially-valued environmental rules and policies. Since the lower part of a building maintains the building's stability and durability, the petroleum companies are represented as fundamental for the implementation of environmental regulations and policies. Nevertheless, the supportive attitude was downplayed by juxtaposing environmental goals with energy goals. The absent information about concrete supportive actions can render an oil company's support symbolic.

ACSRs also used the verb "support" to indicate that the supporting power for environmental solutions comes from governments, businesses, and other stakeholders. In this way, part of the responsibilities of addressing climate change can be transferred to stakeholders and other social groups. By constructing dealing with climate change as a common goal for the oil industry as well as its stakeholders, the potential conflicts between them are reconciled.

The fourth strategy is to use nominalization to construct the concept of support as a real entity so that this concept is less challengeable. When addressing the second research question about gain and loss frames, we found that the source domain BUILDING was used more often as gain frames. The nominal metaphor "support" was often used as gain frames in ACSRs and CCSRs. This metaphor can present the support provided by petroleum companies and the support petroleum companies received as real and necessary. CCSRs tended to use adjectives related to technology to emphasize the technology-oriented approaches to climate change, which were favourable approaches for petroleum companies. Some ACSRs used the nominal metaphor "support" to show closer attention to stakeholders' support, which could be attributable to their publicly-owned nature.

The investigation of topics frequently associated with different interests in CCSRs and ACSRs also indicated how petroleum companies achieve legitimacy by accommodating the various interests of stakeholders. The topic of "Leadership and Management" was used to reconcile the different interests of stakeholders in CCSRs. This topic indicated that mixed interests can be generated by management. One useful way to manage was to build, use, or improve information platforms. By using the metaphor "platform," petroleum companies present the achievements of management as tangible properties for the whole society. As constructing information platforms aligns with China's strong advocacy for information technology, this management approach is thus legitimate according to China's CSR.

As for ACSRs, the topic of "Support and Help" was employed to accommodate the various interests of stakeholders. This topic suggested that different interests can be created with useful assistance or supportive attitudes. In some cases, the support from petroleum companies comes with strings attached, which allows different interests to be reconciled.

Both Chinese and American oil companies legitimize their core business by juxtaposing climate goals with energy demands. However, Chinese oil companies tend to emphasize developing energy to meet domestic demands, as the energy gap in China is relatively wide. American oil companies focus more on global energy demands because the U.S. has become a global energy supplier. These differences also demonstrate different emphases in Chinese and American CSR.

6 Future Work

This study demonstrates the similarities and differences in usages of the BUILDING source domain as gain and loss frames in Chinese and American CSR reports, which paves the way for future research on American and Chinese Corporate Social Responsibility. We also proposed a specific method for identifying gain and loss frames in CSR reports, facilitating the manual annotation of training data for developing an NLP model to automatically detect gain and loss frames in an unlabelled CSR corpus.

References

Aditi Bhatia. 2012. The corporate social responsibility report: The hybridization of a "confused" genre (2007-2011). *IEEE Transactions on Professional Communication*, 55(3), 221–238. https:// 10.1109/TPC.2012.2205732.

Alan J. Richardson and Dowling B. Dowling. 1986. An integrative theory of organizational legitimation. *Scandinavian Journal of Management Studies*, 3, 91–109. https://doi.org/10.1016/0281-7527(86)90022-8

Alexander J. Rothman, Roger D. Bartels, Jhon Wlaschin, and Peter Salovey. 2006. The strategic use of gain- and loss-framed messages to promote healthy behavior: How theory can inform practice. *Journal of Communication*, 56(SUPPL.), 202–220. https://doi.org/10.1111/j.1460-2466.2006.00290.x

Alexander J. Rothman and Peter Salovey. 1997. Shaping perceptions to motivate healthy behavior: The role of message framing. *Psychological Bulletin*, 121(1), 3–19. https://doi.org/10.1037//0033-2909.121.1.3

Amos Tversky and Daniel Kahneman. 1981. The framing of decisions and the psychology of choice. *Science*, 211, 453–458. 10.1126/science.7455683

Andrew Goatly. 2007. *Washing the brain: metaphor and hidden ideology*. Amsterdam Philadelphia: John Benjamins Publishing Co.

Christopher Shaw and Brigitte Nerlich. 2015. Metaphor as a mechanism of global climate change governance: A study of international policies, 1992-2012. *Ecological Economics*, 109, 34–40. https://doi.org/10.1016/j.ecolecon.2014.11.001

Christopher D. Manning, Mihai Surdeanu, John Bauer, Jenny Finkel, Steven J. Bethard, and David McClosky, 2014. The Stanford CoreNLP natural language processing toolkit. In *Proceedings of 52nd Annual Meeting of the Association for Computational Linguistics: System Demonstrations*, pages 55–60.

Dimitrinka Atanasova and Nelya Koteyko. 2017a. Metaphors in Guardian Online and Mail Online Opinion-page Content on Climate Change: War, Religion, and Politics. *Environmental Communication*, 11(4), 452–469. https://doi.org/10.1080/17524032.2015.1024705.

Dimitrinka Atanasova and Nelya Koteyko. 2017b. Metaphors in Online Editorials and Op-Eds about Climate Change, 2006–2013. *The Role of Language in the Climate Change Debate*. Abingdon, Oxon: Routledge. Pages 71–89.

Gerard J. Steen, Aletta G. Dorst, Berenike J. Herrmann, Anna A. Kaal, Tina Krennmayr, and Tryntje Pasma. 2010. *A method for linguistic metaphor identification from MIP to MIPVU*. Amsterdam; Philadelphia: John Benjamins Pub. Co.

Hyunyi Cho and Franklin J. Boster. 2008. Effects of gain versus loss frame antidrug ads on adolescents. *Journal of Communication*, 58(3), 428–446. 10.1111/j.1460-2466.2008.00393.x

Joanna Thornborrow. 1993. Metaphors of security: A comparison of representation in defence discourse in post-cold-war france and britain. *Discourse & Society*. 4(1):99-119. https://doi.org/10.1177/0957926593004001006

Jonathan Charteris-Black. 2005. *Persuasion, legitimacy and leadership. In Politicians and rhetoric: The persuasive power of metaphor*. Hampshire/New York: Palgrave Macmillan.

Jonathan Charteris-Black. 2011. Myth, metaphor and leadership. *Politicians and Rhetoric*. Hampshire/New York: Palgrave Macmillan. Pages 311–329.

Jonathan Charteris-Black. 2004. *Corpus approaches to critical metaphor analysis*. New York: Palgrave Macmillan.

Jonathan Charteris-Black. 2016. *Politicians and Rhetoric: The Persuasive Power of Metaphor*. London: Palgrave Macmillan UK.

Kathleen Ahrens and Menghan Jiang. 2020. Source Domain Verification Using Corpus-based Tools. *Metaphor and Symbol*, 35(1), 43–55. https://doi.org/10.1080/10926488.2020.1712783.

Kathleen Ahrens, Menghan Jiang, and Huiheng Zeng. 2021. building Metaphors in Hong Kong Policy Addresses. *Metaphor in Language and Culture across World Englishes*. London: Bloomsbury Academic. Pages 105-128.

Kristel M. Gallagher and John A. Updegraff. 2012. Health message framing effects on attitudes, intentions, and behavior: A meta-analytic review. *Annals of Behavioral Medicine*, 43(1), 101–116. https://doi.org/10.1007/s12160-011-9308-7.

Louis Wei-Lun Lu and Kathleen Ahrens. 2008. Ideological influence on BUILDING metaphors in Taiwanese presidential speeches. *Discourse and Society*, 19(3), 383–408. https://doi.org/10.1177/0957926508088966.

Mark C. Suchman. 1995. Managing Legitimacy: Strategic and Institutional Approaches. *The Academy of Management Review*, 20(3), 571. https://doi.org/10.2307/258788.

Michael Rundell. 2002. *Macmillan English dictionary for advanced learners*. Oxford: Macmillan.

Paul A. Chilton and Mikhail Ilyin. 1993. Metaphor in political discourse: The case of the 'common european house.' *Discourse & Society*, 4(1), 7–31. https://doi.org/10.1177/0957926593004001002.

Qiang Ji, Ying Fan, Mike Troilo, Ronald D. Ripple, and Lianyong Feng. 2018. China's natural gas demand projections and supply capacity analysis in 2030. *The Energy Journal*, 39(6), 53–70. https://www.jstor.org/stable/26606244.

Reuters. 2021. China's carbon trading scheme makes debut with 4.1 mln T in turnover. Retrieved from https://www.reuters.com/business/sustainable-business/chinas-national-carbon-emission-trading-opens-48-yuant-chinese-media-2021-07-16/.

Shu-Ping Gong, Kathleen Ahrens, and Chu-Ren Huang. 2008. Chinese word sketch and mapping principles: A corpus-based study of conceptual metaphors using the BUILDING source domain. *International Journal of Computer Processing of Languages*, 21(1), 3–17. https://doi.org/10.1142/S1793840608001755.

Siaw-Fong Chung and Chu-Ren Huang. 2010. Using collocations to establish the source domain of conceptual metaphors. *Journal of Chinese Linguistics*, 38(2), 183–223. https://www.jstor.org/stable/23754132.

Sora Kim and Mary Ann T. Ferguson. 2016. Dimensions of effective CSR communication based on public expectation. *Journal of Marketing Communications*. 24 (6), 549-567. 10.1080/13527266.2015.1118143.

Sora Kim and Mary Ann T. Ferguson. 2014. Public expectations of CSR communication: What and how to communicate CSR. *Public Relations Journal*, 8(3).

Suzanne Romaine. 1996. War and Peace in the Global Greenhouse: Metaphors We Die By. *Metaphor and Symbolic Activity*, 11(3), 175–194. https://doi.org/10.1207/s15327868ms1103_1.

Toine van Teeffelen. 1994. Racism and metaphor: The Palestinian-Israeli conflict in popular literature. *Discourse & Society*. 1(1), 91–112. https://doi.org/10.1177/0957926594005003006.

Tony B. Sardinha. 2012. An assessment of metaphor retrieval methods. *Metaphor in use context, culture, and communication*. Amsterdam; Philadelphia: John Benjamins Pub. Co. Pages 31–44.

Kristina Toutanova, Dan Klein, Christopher D. Manning, and Yoram Singer. 2003. Feature-rich part-of-speech tagging with a cyclic dependency network. In *Proceedings of the Conference of the North American Chapter of the Association for Computational Linguistics & Human Language Technologies (NAACL-HLT)*. Pages 252–259.Retrieved from https://aclanthology.org/W03-0900.

U.S. Energy Information Administration. 2018. Today in Energy. Retrieved from https://www.eia.gov/todayinenergy/detail.php?id=37821.

U.S. Energy Information Administration. 2020. Today in Energy. Retrieved from https://www.eia.gov/todayinenergy/detail.php?id=43395.

Yujie Xue. 2022. China's carbon neutral goals: turnover under emissions trading scheme expected to reach US$15 billion in 2030. South China Morning Post. Retrieved from https://www.scmp.com/business/article/3165590/chinas-carbon-neutral-goals-turnover-under-emissions-trading-scheme.

Zha Daojiong. 2006. China's energy security: Domestic and international issues. *Survival*, 48(1), 179–190.

https://doi.org/10.1080/00396330600594322.

Zoltan Kövecses. 2010. *Metaphor: A practical introduction* (2nd ed.). New York: Oxford University Press.

Appendix A.

ACSRs	**CCSRs**
Metaphorical Keywords	**Metaphorical Keywords**
Functions	*Functions*
build *v.* (60), set up *phrasal verb* (4), support *v.* (249), construct *v.* (6), underpin *v.* (3), build up *phrasal verb* (2)	build *v.*(133), set up *phrasal verb* (37), support *v.*(38), construct *v.*(10), repair *v.*(1), build up *phrasal verb* (9)
Qualities	*Qualities*
stable *a.*(11), structural *a.* (2)	stable *a.* (31), structural *a.* (10), supporting *a.*(11)
Entities	*Entities*
support *n.* (70), construction *n.*(3), base *n.* (5), cornerstone *n.*(2), structure *n.* (26), window *n.*(3), home *n.*(4), foundation *n.*(17), door *n.*(1), platform *n.*(3), framework *n.*(82), pillar *n.*(11), building *n.* (2), threshold *n.*(8), barrier *n.*(3)	construction *n.*(36), base *n.*(1), cornerstone *n.*(2), structure *n.*(43), reconstruction *n.*(1), home *n.*(13), foundation *n.*(18), door *n.*(1), platform *n.*(37), framework *n.*(14), pillar *n.*(1), building *n.*(1), support *n.*(28)
Total: 577	**Total: 476**

Table 1. Metaphorical Expressions in the Source Domain of BUILDING

Proceedings of CSR-NLP I @LREC 2022, pages 35–39
Marseille, 25 June 2022

MobASA: Corpus for Aspect-based Sentiment Analysis and Social Inclusion in the Mobility Domain

Aleksandra Gabryszak, Philippe Thomas
Deutsches Forschungszentrum für Künstliche Intelligenz
Alt-Moabit 91c, 10559 Berlin, Germany
{aleksandra.gabryszak, philippe.thomas}@dfki.de

Abstract

In this paper we show how aspect-based sentiment analysis might help public transport companies to improve their social responsibility for accessible travel. We present `MobASA`: a novel German-language corpus of tweets annotated with their relevance for public transportation, and with sentiment towards aspects related to barrier-free travel. We identified and labeled topics important for passengers limited in their mobility due to disability, age, or when travelling with young children. The data can be used to identify hurdles and improve travel planning for vulnerable passengers, as well as to monitor a perception of transportation businesses regarding the social inclusion of all passengers. The data is publicly available under: https://github.com/DFKI-NLP/sim3s-corpus

Keywords: Aspect-based Sentiment Analysis, Crowdsourcing, Mobility, Social Inclusion, Social Responsibility

1. Introduction

Social inclusion is of great importance for building stable societies and public transportation companies play a particularly substantial role for ensuring equal participation in society. Unfortunately, accessing trains, buses, or stations is often a challenge for people limited in their mobility due to a physical or cognitive impairment, age or when travelling with young children. It is important to enable those groups to use public transport in a self-reliant way by providing facilities (lifts or ramps for walking disabled people, etc.), services (visual info for deaf and acoustic info for blind people, etc.), as well as systems informing about the state of these forms of assistance (if lifts are available, etc.) in order to identify unexpected hurdles and improve travel planning. Natural language processing provides means to aid such systems by the automatic extraction of information from texts about the condition of relevant facilities and services. For example, given the input text:

> *A lift at the Berlin Hbf station has been already defect for two days! This is really annoying!*

it would be helpful to have a system that is able to determine that (a) the availability of lifts at public transportation stations is mentioned and (b) their state is described as malfunctioning. The extracted information can be used to inform transport operators as well as passengers limited in their mobility about a problem of a specific facility, trigger a process solving or mitigating the problem (e.g. fixing broken lifts, proposing an alternative traveling route).

In this paper we devote our attention to the question of supporting such systems by adapting the aspect-based sentiment analysis task. Sentiment analysis aims at extracting and quantifying subjective information. A standard version of the sentiment detection classifies the sentiment of a whole sentence, while the aspect-based sentiment analysis (ABSA) focuses on the sentiment towards predefined aspects such as specific products or services. Therefore, ABSA allows a more fine-grained mining of opinions. We cast our problem of extracting information on the state of facilities and services relevant to the barrier-free accessibility of public transport as an aspect-based sentiment task. We consider facilities and services as main aspects, their properties as aspect subcategories, and statements about those properties as phrases potentially expressing or implying a sentiment. For the example above, we assume a main category *lift*, a subcategory *availability* (of the lift), and a negative sentiment towards the aspect *Lift#Availability*.

As a result of our work we present `MobASA`, a German-language dataset for the detection of sentiment towards aspects relevant for users of public transport limited in their mobility. To the best of our knowledge there is no other dataset, English or German, which covers the topic of travel accessibility in a fine-grained way. Our contributions are:

- We provide a publicly available German-language dataset for the detection of aspect-based sentiment towards barrier-related aspects in the public transport domain.
- The dataset can benefit building inclusive public transportation systems as described in the introduction. Therefore, we add to research aiming to deploy various NLP tasks in support of equality and social responsibility of businesses.

2. Related Work

Aspect-based Sentiment The annotated datasets for developing ABSA models are still scarce, and they mostly cover only the standard domain of product or service reviews (e.g. SCARE corpus by (Sänger et al., 2016), SemEval 2015 by (Pontiki et al., 2015), USAGE by (Klinger and Cimiano, 2014), GESTALT by (Ruppenhofer et al., 2014)). In contrast, the GermEval 2017 dataset (Wojatzki et al., 2017) comprises social media texts annotated with opinions on the biggest railway company in Germany. It lists barrier-free accessibility as one coarse-grain aspect, however more refined labels are needed to model information needs of different target groups (e.g. blind vs. deaf people).

Recent neural approaches based on pre-trained language models (e.g., BERT (Devlin et al., 2019)) have shown impressive results for the task when fine-tuned on supervised datasets. However, the state-of-the-art transformer based ABSA models currently achieve an F1-score of only 0.53 on the GermEval 2017 dataset (Aßenmacher et al., 2021) and 0.61 on the SemEval 2016 laptop-dataset (Pontiki et al., 2016; Li et al., 2019), for example, meaning there is still much room for improvement.

Inclusive NLP Natural language processing (NLP) technologies already support the efforts of inclusion in various domains, for example, sign-language-to-text translation systems (Nunnari et al., 2021) to benefit deaf people, domain-specific translation systems to support migrants when communicating with authorities (Xu et al., 2018), as well as applications predicting readability to help content providers with adjusting their published texts to the needs of people with cognitive disabilities (Evans et al., 2016). The systems target mostly language and communication barriers.

3. Dataset

3.1. Data Collection

To collect the relevant data we crawled German-language tweets based on a predefined list of 11 Twitter channels of public transportation companies, channels related to barrier-free accessibility as well as a set of 68 keywords relevant to the barrier-free travel of handicapped passengers, older people or parents with small children. The list contained German-language keywords equivalent to words such as: *barrier-free, escalator, guiding system for the blind*, etc. We collected 3,128,639 tweets between 2019-2021, and from that data we sampled tweets for the annotation.

3.2. Annotation Schema and Guidelines

The MobASA labels structure and annotation guidelines are partly based on the instructions of GermEval 2017 and SemEval 2015 datasets. The set of meta-labels (relevance, sentiment, category, polarity, from, to) as well as the XML data format originate from GermEval 2017.

Relevance for Public Transportation Each tweet has binary labelling regarding its `relevance` to public transport. The relevance value is *true*, if a tweet contains any phrase related to public passenger transport of any type. For example, the text in Figure 1 contains mentions of a metro station.

Aspect-based Sentiment We defined a base catalog of 19 aspect `categories` relevant to the barrier-free travel. We included aspects important for the walking disabled passengers, people with a vision or hearing impairment, as well as the elderly, and parents traveling with small children. The category catalog is based on interviews with those target groups, guidelines for travel accessibility by the government and interest groups, information provided by the biggest German railway operator, as well as topics mentioned in our data. Each aspect category consists of two parts: a main aspect and its subcategory. The main aspect references mostly a specific assistance form (facility or service) such as lift, lighting or acoustic info. The subcategory captures various relevant features of the main aspect such as its availability among others. The subcategory might also be labelled *Main* if no multiple, specific subcategories are identified. We defined up to two subcategories for each aspect. The category *Others* was annotated if an unanticipated or less frequent but relevant topic was not covered in the base catalog. For example, very short-term announcements of platform changes for departing trains might result in people impaired in their mobility missing their train. Examples of the annotation of various subcategories for tweets, which referenced a main aspect are given in Table 2.

Furthermore, each aspect is annotated along with a `polarity` value *neutral*, *positive* or *negative*. The value indicates either stated sentiment towards an aspect or, more broadly, it indicates the described state of that aspect. For example, the polarity of the category *GeneralBarrier#Main* is usually positive if a station or a train is stated as being handicapped accessible, negative if it is not, and neutral if the degree of accessibility is stated as unknown or is described as neither positive nor negative for other reasons. The texts might contain opinionated statements such as *bad* or *good*, however, this is not required, i.e we also accept polarities implied by the state of the aspect (e.g. a faulty lift implies a negative polarity as in the example in Figure 1).

Furthermore, we asked to annotate the value regarding the most recent described or announced state of the aspect, i.e. if the lighting was faulty, but it is stated as already repaired, then the sentiment is positive. This approach was chosen with the aim in mind to support systems which focus on solving the latest problems when using public transport.

The `target` of an annotated aspect and its polarity is a text span referencing the main aspect, e.g. phrases *Aufzug* denoting the main aspect *Lift*. The offsets of the target span are marked by the labels `from` and `to`.

Document-level Sentiment Each tweet is labeled with a document-level `sentiment`. Its value aggregates the polarities of the opinions in a given text. If the polarity set is {*positive*, *neutral*} or {*negative*, *neutral*} then the document-level sentiment is set to positive or negative, respectively, otherwise the value is *neutral* (as illustrated by the example in Figure 1). If a text is irrelevant, then the document-level sentiment is *neutral* by default.[1]

3.3. Annotation process and quality

Expert annotation A subset of tweets is fully annotated by trained experts using the platform *Inception*[2]. The final expert subset of the corpus includes only annotations, for which two annotators agreed or the disagreement was resolved by the third annotator. The annotation is based on guidelines, which were developed in an iterative process and take into account discussions with the experts. The annotators were given definitions of relevance and the aspects along with multiple examples. The annotation of aspect-

[1] We follow in our approach the heuristic used in GermEval2017 data.

[2] https://inception-project.github.io/

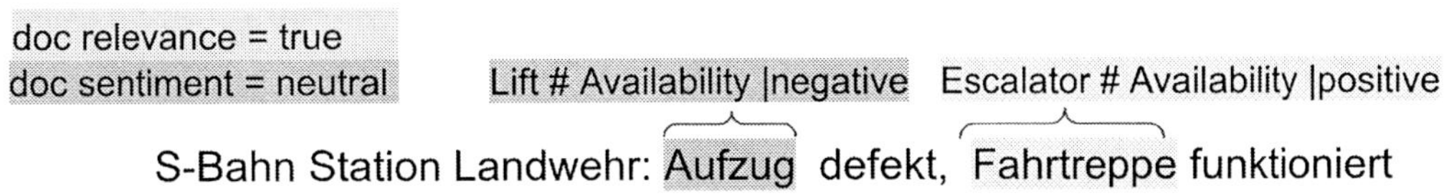

Figure 1: Example of a German-language tweet relevant for public transportation and containing negative sentiment towards the aspect *Lift#Availability* and positive sentiment towards the aspect *Escalator#Availability*. (Text in EN: *S-Bahn Station Landwehr: Lift defect, Escalator is working.*)

aspect	description
AccidentsMobilityGroups#Main	risks of injury for people with limited mobility (e.g. falls of wheelchair users into track bed)
AcousticSignal#Main	acoustic signals for blind people (acoustic warning or signals for finding train doors, etc.)
ConstructionSite#Main	construction sites and their impact on the public transport (e.g. accessing of stations)
Demonstration#Main	demonstrations and their impact on the public transport (e.g. accessing of stations)
Escalator#Availability	operational status of escalators (e.g. if they exist and function properly)
Escalator#Tidiness	cleanliness of escalators (also smell or similar)
GeneralBarrier#Main	general mentions of barrier-free accessibility in public transport
GroundLevelAccess#Main	ground level access to stations or vehicles of public transport
InfoAcoustic#Availability	availability of announcements or operational state of loudspeakers
InfoDisplay#Availability	availability of displayed information or operational state of display boards
Info#Others	availability and quality of information on public transport in apps, e-mails, etc.
Lift#Availability	operational status of lifts
Lift#Tidiness	cleanliness of lifts (also smell or similar)
Lighting#Availability	operational status of lighting
Ramp#Availability	operational status of ramps
Security#Main	security at stations (e.g. important for older or handicapped people)
SpaceMobilityGroups#Main	space available for people limited in their mobility (e.g. wheelchair bay)
TactileContrastOrientation#Main	tactile or high-contrast guiding routes for blind people, info in braille, etc.
main category#Others	not anticipated or less frequent subcategories (e.g. InfoDisplay#Others for correctness of displayed info)
BarrierOthers#Main	other topics related to barrier-free accessibility (e.g. assistance during traveling)

Table 1: Definition of aspect categories related to barrier-free accessibility

based sentiment was only considered for the data annotated as relevant. The inner-annotator agreement for the various annotation layers is: 1) relevance: Cohen's $\kappa = 0.96$, 2) aspect-based sentiment: Cohen's $\kappa = 0.73$ on annotated tokens only. Therefore we achieved nearly perfect agreement in the relevance annotation and substantial agreement in the aspect-based sentiment annotation.

Crowdsourcing An additional subset of tweets was annotated by crowdworkers using the platform *Crowdee*[3]. First, the workers labelled tweets as relevant or irrelevant for the public transportation topic. Subsequently, the tweets were annotated regarding aspect-based sentiment. In order to choose relevant candidates for the aspect annotation, first we sampled tweets already labeled or automatically determined as relevant for public transportation. For the automatic detection we systematically collected phrases referring to transportation types from a subset of relevant tweets, and used those phrases to filter the potentially relevant data. In the next step we automatically pre-annotated text spans with the main aspect category (e.g. word *Fahrstuhl* with main category `Lift`) by matching text spans to target strings annotated in the expert subset. Then we showed crowdworkers texts, where a pre-annotated main aspects were highlighted, and we asked if a specific subcategory regarding the highlighted aspect is discussed in a given text, and if so with which polarity. The task was designed as a multiple-choice questionnaire. For the crowdsourcing we focused on aspects most relevant to various target groups (e.g. *Escalator#Availability*), and excluded rare or less relevant aspects (e.g. *TactileContrastOrientation#Main*, *Lift#Tidiness*). For the annotation of both tasks we provided short guidelines as well as many examples. Each tweet was processed by two workers. To ensure a higher quality of the crowdsourcing process we prepared a qualification test, inserted trapping questions, and set a minimum time for solving the task. We blocked all users, who failed the tests from further tasks. Finally we included only annotations, for which two workers agreed on. We reviewed a sample of the crowd-sourced labels included in the final data. We estimated the accuracy of the relevance labels as very high having 99.6% correct labels of 1000 sampled tweets. Regarding aspect-based sentiment we reviewed 1950 answers and estimate the accuracy as high based on the 84.9% correct labels.

3.4. Data Statistics

We provide dev and test split as well as two versions of the train set (Table 3). The dev and test and train$_{\text{BASE}}$ split contain data, in which all relevant tweets are annotated by the experts, and the irrelevant data is partially labeled by the crowdworkers. We also publish an extended version of the train corpus, train$_{\text{PLUS}}$, which additionally contains the

[3] https://www.crowdee.com/

aspect	polarity	example
InfoDisplay#Availability	neutral	*Sag mir mal, wenn es geht, ob die Anzeigetafeln am Hbf wieder gehen!* :D *(Tell me if the displayboards at the main station are working again! :D)*
InfoDisplay#Availability	positive	*Die Anzeigetafeln am Hauptbahnhof Bremen laufen wieder* *(The displayboards at Bremen Central Station are functioning again)*
InfoDisplay#Availability	negative	*S2 08:02 ab Bernau fährt nicht weil? [...] keine Anzeige.* Scheiße! *(S2 08:02 from Bernau is not coming because? [...] no info displayed. Crap!)*
InfoDisplay#Others	negative	*Sbahn fällt 3x aus, [...] schrift auf anzeigetafle ist verkehrt herum* *(Sbahn canceled 3x time, [...] text on displayboard is upside down)*
(no relevant aspect)	-	*@jbnieo Komm mit der Bahn so um 12.06 an, lass uns dann bei der Anzeigetafel treffen.* *(@jbnieo Arrive by train around 12.06, then let's meet at the displayboard.)*

Table 2: Examples of the annotation of texts containing the main aspect *InfoDisplay* (original texts and English translations)

crowd-sourced annotations of the aspect-based sentiment.

The inclusion of primarily expert annotation in dev and test set ensures a more robust selection and evaluation of the models, since the expert annotation introduces less noisy labels. That approach follows the suggestions of a careful design of the test data to not misrepresent model performance (Alt et al., 2020; Bowman and Dahl, 2021).

	total	dev	test	$train_{BASE}$	$train_{PLUS}$
docs	29446	4176	4192	12510	21078
relevant	18378	1960	1899	5951	14519
aspects	13533	1205	1150	3572	11178

Table 3: Statistics of the data splits

Relevance The binary relevance labels are relatively equally distributed in dev, test and $train_{BASE}$ (Table 3). In $train_{PLUS}$ the relevant docs are dominant, since we selected only relevant classes for the crowdsourcing of aspect annotation. Therefore, the second split should primarily be used for the detection of aspect-based sentiment.

Aspect and Sentiment Table 4 shows 10 most frequent aspects. For some main concepts such as *TactileContrastOrientation* for blind people we almost found no data. In contrast, other main aspects such as *InfoAcoustic* or *Escalator* are often mentioned in text, however not in a context relevant to barrier-free accessibility. Also subcategories such as *Tidiness* of lifts or escalators are rarely mentioned.

Table 5 shows the distribution of document-level and aspect-level sentiment values. The neutral values build the majority of classes on the document-level, however it is due to the annotation of irrelevant tweets with neutral sentiment as default. For the relevant data negative sentiment is the most dominant on document- and span-level. We also observed, that mostly the expressed sentiment refers to the current or past state of the aspect. However for the category *GeneralBarrier#Main* the positive sentiment often refers to the future state, e.g. the future barrier-free accessibility of stations is announced.

aspect	total	expert	crowd
GeneralBarrier#Main	3010	807	2203
Lift#Availability	2918	1586	1332
Escalator#Availability	1615	769	846
InfoDisplay#Availability	1545	351	1194
ConstructionSite#Main	1069	103	966
Lighting#Availability	786	509	277
InfoAcoustic#Availability	686	231	455
Ramp#Availability	434	101	333
InfoDisplay#Others	349	349	0
Demonstration#Main	232	232	0
others	889	889	0
total	13533	5927	7606

Table 4: Statistics of 10 most frequent aspect categories

polarity	doc level	span level
neutral	19660	1652
positive	1968	2361
negative	7818	9520
total	29446	13533

Table 5: Statistics of the aspect-based sentiment

4. Conclusion and Future Work

Most of the inclusive NLP systems focus on overcoming communication barriers. In contrast, we show how NLP can be used by public transportation businesses to mitigate barriers resulting from broken travel facilities or services, and in result to support inclusion of all passengers. We presented a corpus of tweets annotated with sentiment towards aspects related to barrier-free travel. In future work, we want to refine the aspect catalog, and integrate the detection of aspect location and time, to which the sentiment refers.

5. Acknowledgements

This research was partially supported by the Federal Ministry of Transport and Digital Infrastructure (BMVI) through the project SIM3S (19F2058B) and by the German Federal Ministry of Education and Research (BMBF) through the project BIFOLD (01IS18025E).

6. Bibliographical References

Alt, C., Gabryszak, A., and Hennig, L. (2020). TACRED revisited: A thorough evaluation of the TACRED relation extraction task. *CoRR*, abs/2004.14855.

Aßenmacher, M., Corvonato, A., and Heumann, C. (2021). Re-evaluating germeval17 using german pre-trained language models. In *Proceedings of the Swiss Text Analytics Conference 2021*.

Bowman, S. R. and Dahl, G. E. (2021). What will it take to fix benchmarking in natural language understanding? *CoRR*, abs/2104.02145.

Devlin, J., Chang, M.-W., Lee, K., and Toutanova, K. (2019). BERT: Pre-training of deep bidirectional transformers for language understanding. In *Proceedings of the 2019 Conference of the North American Chapter of the Association for Computational Linguistics: Human Language Technologies, Volume 1 (Long and Short Papers)*, pages 4171–4186, Minneapolis, Minnesota, June. Association for Computational Linguistics.

Evans, R., Yaneva, V., and Temnikova, I. (2016). Predicting reading difficulty for readers with autism spectrum disorder.

Klinger, R. and Cimiano, P. (2014). The USAGE review corpus for fine grained multi lingual opinion analysis. In *Proceedings of the Ninth International Conference on Language Resources and Evaluation (LREC'14)*, pages 2211–2218, Reykjavik, Iceland, May. European Language Resources Association (ELRA).

Li, X., Bing, L., Zhang, W., and Lam, W. (2019). Exploiting BERT for end-to-end aspect-based sentiment analysis. In *Proceedings of the 5th Workshop on Noisy User-generated Text (W-NUT 2019)*, pages 34–41, Hong Kong, China, November. Association for Computational Linguistics.

Nunnari, F., España-Bonet, C., and Avramidis, E. (2021). A data augmentation approach for sign-language-to-text translation in-the-wild. In *Proceedings of the 3rd Conference on Language, Data and Knowledge. Conference on Language, Data and Knowledge (LDK-2021), September 1-4, Zaragoza/Hybrid, Spain*, volume 93 of *OpenAccess Series in Informatics (OASIcs)*. Dagstuhl publishing, 9.

Pontiki, M., Galanis, D., Papageorgiou, H., Manandhar, S., and Androutsopoulos, I. (2015). SemEval-2015 task 12: Aspect based sentiment analysis. In *Proceedings of the 9th International Workshop on Semantic Evaluation (SemEval 2015)*, pages 486–495, Denver, Colorado, June. Association for Computational Linguistics.

Pontiki, M., Galanis, D., Papageorgiou, H., Androutsopoulos, I., Manandhar, S., AL-Smadi, M., Al-Ayyoub, M., Zhao, Y., Qin, B., De Clercq, O., Hoste, V., Apidianaki, M., Tannier, X., Loukachevitch, N., Kotelnikov, E., Bel, N., Jiménez-Zafra, S. M., and Eryiğit, G. (2016). SemEval-2016 task 5: Aspect based sentiment analysis. In *Proceedings of the 10th International Workshop on Semantic Evaluation (SemEval-2016)*, pages 19–30, San Diego, California, June. Association for Computational Linguistics.

Ruppenhofer, J., Klinger, R., Struß, J. M., Sonntag, J., and Wiegand, M. (2014). Iggsa shared tasks on german sentiment analysis (gestalt).

Sänger, M., Leser, U., Kemmerer, S., Adolphs, P., and Klinger, R. (2016). SCARE — the sentiment corpus of app reviews with fine-grained annotations in German. In *Proceedings of the Tenth International Conference on Language Resources and Evaluation (LREC'16)*, pages 1114–1121, Portorož, Slovenia, May. European Language Resources Association (ELRA).

Wojatzki, M., Ruppert, E., Holschneider, S., Zesch, T., and Biemann, C. (2017). GermEval 2017: Shared Task on Aspect-based Sentiment in Social Media Customer Feedback. In *Proceedings of the GermEval 2017 Shared Task on Aspect-based Sentiment in Social Media Customer Feedback*, pages 1–12, Berlin, Germany.

Xu, F., Uszkoreit, H., Schmeier, S., and Ayach, A. (2018). Fahum heißt verstehen: Eine flüchtlings-app für soforthilfe und integration. In Aljoscha Burchardt et al., editors, *IT für soziale Inklusion: Digitalisierung – Künstliche Intelligenz – Zukunft für alle*, pages 151–154. De Gruyter Oldenbourg.

Proceedings of CSR-NLP I @LREC 2022, pages 40–45
Marseille, 25 June 2022

Detecting Violation of Human Rights via Social Media

Yash Pilankar, Rejwanul Haque, Mohammed Hasanuzzaman, Paul Stynes, Pramod Pathak
School of Computing
National College of Ireland
Mayor Street Lower, IFSC, Dublin 1, Ireland
x19216858@student.ncirl.ie, firstname.lastname@ncirl.ie

Abstract

Social media is not just meant for entertainment, it provides platforms for sharing information, news, facts and events. In the digital age, activists and numerous users are seen to be vocal regarding human rights and their violations in social media. However, their voices do not often reach to the targeted audience and concerned human rights organization. In this work, we aimed at detecting factual posts in social media about violation of human rights in any part of the world. The end product of this research can be seen as an useful assest for different peacekeeping organizations who could exploit it to monitor real-time circumstances about any incident in relation to violation of human rights. We chose one of the popular micro-blogging websites, Twitter, for our investigation. We used supervised learning algorithms in order to build human rights violation identification (HRVI) models which are able to identify Tweets in relation to incidents of human right violation. For this, we had to manually create a data set, which is one of the contributions of this research. We found that our classification models that were trained on this gold-standard dataset performed excellently in classifying factual Tweets about human rights violation, achieving an accuracy of upto 93% on hold-out test set.

Keywords: Human Rights Violation, Fact Checking, Machine Learning

1. Introduction

Over the last two decades, we have seen astounding growth and development across a wide range of disciplines including science and technology, and the adaptation of modern ideologies has significantly accelerated the growth of every nation. However, there are still many locations around the world, where people do not even enjoy basic human rights and freedoms. In current affairs, there have been countless situations befalling around the world, where human rights are continuously being violated, and unfortunately these incidents go unnoticed. Activists across the world aim to bring such issues to light as soon as they become aware of such incidents. Likewise, media reporters and activists are on field risking their lives to cover such incidents and bring them in front of the world. We refer the readers to one recent heartbreaking incident that was reported by Laskar and Sunny (2021) in Hindustan Times. It is regarding Danish Siddiqui,[1] India's one of most renowned and Pulitzer prize-winning photojournalists, who was reportedly killed while reporting an instance where human rights were being violated. Russia's invasion of Ukraine is the world's centre of attention today, and the escalation in violations of human rights law, including deaths of civilians resulting from unlawful attacks are being reported everyday.

Over the past few years, we have seen many crowd-sourced technological solutions, one of which is Ushahidi.[2] It is a map-based tracker that is used to monitor event-based situation and tags the location over the map. Similarly, Syria Tracker[3] is a tool that is used for reporting incidents about human rights abuse and tag the location of the incidents in map so that its neighborhoods become aware about the situation.

There have been a staggering growth and usage of micro-blogging platforms since the beginning of this century. In fact, social media has become one of the mediums, where people raise voices for human rights and tend to share factual and truthful events occurring nearby for justice. Over the past decade, NLP researchers both from academia or industry investigated sentiment analysis by analyzing data from a variety of micro-blogging websites. However, significant portion of these works aimed at identifying characteristics or opinions of user-generated content such as users' emotions, intentions, mood, behaviors and sentiments (Neethu and Rajasree, 2013; Waseem and Hovy, 2016; Haque et al., 2019; Singh et al., 2020a; Singh et al., 2020b). Recently, Alhelbawy et al. (2020) developed a HRVI platform for Arabic to monitor human rights violation in several countries in Central Asia. For this, they built Naïve Bayes and Support Vector Machine (SVM) classifiers on tweet data. As in Alhelbawy et al. (2020), we focused in detecting human rights violation in Tweets. Unlike Arabic as in Alhelbawy et al. (2020), we considered English Tweets for our investigation so that incidents about human right violations worldwide can be traced.

More specifically, in this work, we focused on identifying "factual" information from Tweets rather than

[1] `https://en.wikipedia.org/wiki/Danish_Siddiqui`

[2] `https://www.ushahidi.com/`

[3] `https://syriatracker.crowdmap.com/`

categorising opinionated Tweets. In order to do this, we crawled Tweets in relation to events and incidents about human right violations. Then, we made use these Tweets in order to create a gold-standard dataset which is used to build and evaluate our HRVI classifiers. Everyday thousands of social media posts about entertainment or so become viral; however, posts about human rights violation are not seen, cornered, and does not reach to the targeted audience. Our work aims at aiding organizations whose intention is to keep peace and harmony within the nations and society by tracking situation and incidents in relation to human right violations. We employed a number of machine learning (ML) algorithms in order to build our HRVI classification models. Our expectation was that our HRVI systems would be able to identify specific factual Tweets. One of the main contributions of this work is the creation of the gold-standard data for the HRVI task, which, we believe, could serve as an invaluable asset as far as this line of NLP research is concerned. To the best of our knowledge, there is no readily available dataset that one can freely use for HRVI via social media platforms. We also believe that our work would not only advance NLP research but also have positive societal and political impacts.

2. Related Works

For sentiment analysis gathering relevant dataset has always been a challenge but can be collected following a set of standard methods, e.g. crawling, scrapping and REST API. Jiang et al. (2017) used scrapping technique for getting microblogs from Sina.[4] Twitter is one of the most widely-used social media platforms in the world and one can use its API to easily to fetch and crawl millions of Tweets. Waseem and Hovy (2016) created a corpus mainly on hatespeech by collecting over 130K Tweets using Twitter API. Likewise, Davidson et al. (2017) collected a set of Tweets (25K) in order to create a corpus for hatespeech. Further, in order to produce a gold-standard data for their task, Waseem and Hovy (2016) prepared a set of rules which were used in their annotation task. They ended up with a dataset containing 16K Tweets. In case of Davidson et al. (2017), they performed the annotation task with the help of CrowdFlower[5] users.

Unlike the strategy described above, Zahoor and Rohilla (2020) took a different approach for annotation as they utilized TextBlob, a NLP library, for getting sentiment (i.e. positive, negative and neutral) of posts. Neethu and Rajasree (2013) proposed a simple method for creating lexical feature vector for collecting Tweets from Twitter, and their annotation task was performed manually. Hamdan et al. (2015) used feature extraction methods such as polarity score over ten different lexicon along with a slang dictionary of Twitter for handling social media post containing slang. Lim et al. (2020) used features from pre-trained language model (Embedding from Language Models (ELMo)), and Term Frequency–Inverse Document Frequency (TF-IDF). Interestingly, they observed that use of parts-of-speech (PoS) feature does not help in classification of micro-blog texts.

Event-based sentiment classification was one of the important turnarounds regarding 2016 Presidential Election in United States. Somula et al. (2020) performed an experiment taking Tweets posted during that time into account for the prediction of the election winner. The event-based sentiment classification has also been been adopted in different campaigns. For example, Fitri et al. (2019) performed predictive analysis on anti-LGBTQ campaign in Indonesia. The similar strategy was also taken into account for monitoring human rights abuse in Iraq (Alhelbawy et al., 2020). Alhelbawy et al. (2020) developed a map-based platform called Ceasefire[6] that reports location where any human rights were violated. It also offers a feature that fetches Tweets from Twitter about any human rights abuse and tags the locations mentioned in the Tweets. As the portal was specifically developed for peace in Iraq, it was limited to Arabic only. Alhelbawy et al. (2020) used vector space learning technique for text, i.e. word2vec (Mikolov et al., 2013), and TF-IDF method for weighted scheme. They tested a number of ML techniques and algorithms (e.g. Linear SVM, Gaussian SVM and Naïve Bayes) in their task, and achieved the highest accuracy when they applied the combination of CNN and LSTM.

As for sentiment analysis, there have been a plethora of works that studied this area of NLP considering both high-resource and low-resource languages. We refer the interested readers some of the notable works (Lim et al., 2020; Kanakaraddi et al., 2020; Qin et al., 2020) who investigated sentiment analysis using more advanced ML techniques such as bidirectional encoder representations from Transformers (BERT) (Devlin et al., 2018a).

3. Experimental Setups

3.1. Collecting Tweets

To the best of our knowledge, there is no publicly available dataset for HRVI task. For this, we created a gold-standard data set for this task. We used Twitter API, Tweepy,[7] in order to collect Tweets. We are interested in collecting those Tweets which would be relevant for the task. This is in fact a challenging and time-consuming task. One of the ways is to collect Tweets from those Twitter accounts which are reliable and post

[4] https://en.wikipedia.org/wiki/Sina_Weibo

[5] https://en.wikipedia.org/wiki/Figure_Eight_Inc.

[6] http://iraq.ceasefire.org/

[7] https://docs.tweepy.org/en/stable/api.html

Tweets on subjective matters such as human rights violation. We looked at the profiles of various NGOs and peace-maker organizations, e.g. Human Rights Watch, Amnesty, United Nations, and Refugees, and came up with a list of relevant Twitter accounts. We also looked at personal Twitter profiles of many activists, e.g. Malala Yousafzai, Nadia Murad, who have been vocal over human rights and their violation. In sum, we collected those Twitter account names that are related to the context of human rights and violations of human rights, which are required for the creation of our dataset. Finally, we used Tweepy with the list of user accounts and collected Tweets. Our second approach is based on search query functionality available in Tweepy. We turned on language filtering functionality and set it to English. This does not consider Tweets of non-English languages. We also turned on filtering for RetTweets in order to avoid them. This helped in removing redundant Tweets. Lastly, we supplied a list of search keywords such as "child abuse", "ban on education", "attack on civilians". Using the two above approaches we collected a list of 15,590 Tweets which are considered for the annotation task (cf. Section 3.2).

3.2. Annotation Process

This section describes our data annotation process. In Section 2, we talked about different data annotation methods for the sentiment classification tasks. Our task is identification of human rights violation through social media posts. In short, it is a binary classification task where given a Tweet it checks whether there is any incident about human rights violation. We labelled a Tweet with "1" when we see that it contains information, event, fact or incident about human rights violation. The concerned Tweet may also contain location where the incident occurred. The additional clues that we considered for tagging were: (i) there may be a victim such as any community, person, group of people, and (ii) information about the assailant who violated the rights. The dataset that we created is different from the existing sentiment analysis tasks, where sentiments such as feelings and opinions of the user are checked based on content of the post alone. In our case, it is more focused on facts that is encoded in the Tweet. In sum, we labeled each of the collected clean Tweets with either one of the two categories: '1' (indicating the violation of human rights), '0' (normal post that does not indicate any violation of human rights). Note that since data annotation is an expensive and time-consuming task, we had only single annotator for this task, who is a native speaker of English and has excellent knowledge in Tweets or micro blogs.

On completion of annotation task, we ended up with a list of 10,077 annotated Tweets. Figure 1 shows the distribution of these instances in each class ('1' and '0'). As can be seen from Figure 1, this is a highly imbalanced dataset. We see that the number of instances of the minority class ('1': indicating human rights violation) is 1,057, and the same of the majority class is 9,020 ('0': indicating no human rights violation). We split the data set into two parts: train and test sets. The train and test sets contain 7,557 and 2,520 instances, respectively.

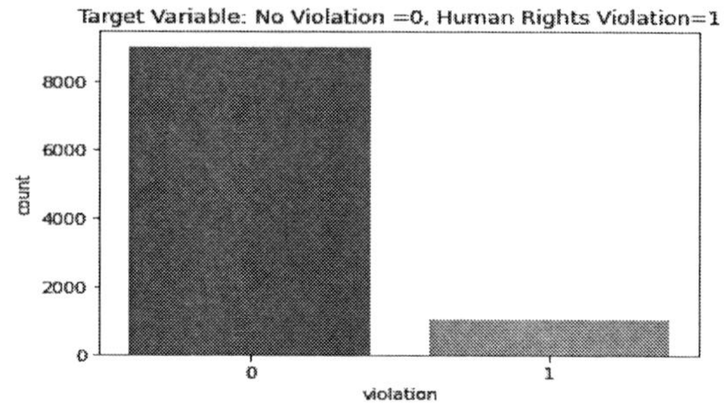

Figure 1: Class Distribution.

3.3. Quality of Annotation

At the end of the annotation task, each tweet is associated with one of the two tags: '1' or '0'. Since we have one annotator, one value is associated with each of the 10,077 Tweets. In order to measure how good annotation process was, a set of 200 Tweets were randomly sampled from the data set such that they are equally distributed across the both classes, and annotated by another annotator. The second annotator who only annotated this small set of Tweets (200) were instructed with the annotation guidelines that were given to the first annotator. On completion of this annotation task, we computed inter-annotator agreement using Fleiss' Kappa (Fleiss and Cohen, 1973) at Tweet level. For each tweet, we count an agreement whenever two annotators agree with the annotation result. We found the Kappa score to be high (i.e. 0.90) for the annotation task. This indicates that our tweet labeling task is to be excellent in quality.

3.4. Overview on our HRVI Systems

Figure 2 illustrates the working architecture of our HRVI system. Each of the components of the HRVI model is clearly shown in Figure 2, and they are placed under three different layers: data layer, logical layer and client layer. The data layer includes tasks such as data collection, cleaning and annotation. Spacy,[8] an open-source software library for advanced natural language processing, is used for data cleaning. It also took into account abbreviations, slangs, #tags, links, user tags, and provided us a clean data. We performed tonenisation, stop word removal and encoding (word embedding) based on the requirements of our learning algorithms. TF-IDF weighting is used for classical machine learning algorithms, i.e. random forest (RF), support vector machine (SVM)). RF is an extension of Bagging technique, which includes subspace sampling

[8]https://spacy.io/

strategy. Hyperparameters for the RF classifier were tuned using GridSearchCV,[9] a hyperparameter search technique using cross validation. As for SVM, we used the default set of hyperparameters of Scikit-learn[10] for our experiments.

Vaswani et al. (2017) introduced Transformer as an efficient alternative to recurrent or convolutional neural networks. Based on the Transformer architecture, Devlin et al. (2018b) proposed a powerful NN architecture – BERT – for a variety of NLP tasks including text classification such as sentiment analysis. BERT is a multi-layer bidirectional Transformer encoder architecture which provides context-aware representations from an unlabeled text by jointly conditioning from both the left and right contexts within a sentence. It can also be used as a pre-trained model with one additional output layer to fine-tune downstream NLP tasks, such as sentiment analysis, and natural language inferencing. For fine-tuning, the BERT model is first initialized with the pre-trained parameters, and all of the parameters are fine-tuned using the labeled data from the downstream tasks. There were two steps in BERT training: *pre-training* and *fine-tuning*. During pre-training, the model is trained on unlabeled data. As for fine-tuning, it is first initialized with the pre-trained parameters, and all of the parameters are fine-tuned using the labeled data from the downstream tasks (e.g. sentiment analysis). This strategy has been successfully applied to different fact checking tasks in social media (e.g. Williams et al. (2020)). In this work, we also investigated human rights violation identification in social media sphere using BERT.

4. Results and Discussion

In order to evaluate our HRVI models, we used metrics that are widely used for evaluating classifiers, i.e. accuracy, recall, precision and F1. In Table 1, we show the performance of our classifiers in terms of these metrics. As can be seen from Table 1, RF and SVM performed excellently in the task. BERT produces a moderate performance (an F1 of 0.80 and 75% accuracy on the test data).

	Acc	Precision	Recall	F1
RF	0.93	0.93	0.93	0.92
SVM	0.93	0.93	0.93	0.92
BERT	0.75	0.91	0.75	0.80

Table 1: Performance of our HRVI models.

We also show their performance using confusion matrix, which provides more insights on how they perform on each class. In Figure 3, we show confusion matrix for the RF classifier. As can be seen from Figure 3, RF is able to classify most of the test set instances correctly. However, it misclassified 161 instances of the positive class, i.e. they were incorrectly classified as normal Tweets ('0') (i.e. false negative (FN)). In sum, it performed poorly on the positive class (i.e. true-positive rate (TPR): 103 / 264 = 39.01%), and we are mainly interested in that class.

We show confusion matrix for SVM in Figure 4. We obtained a slightly improved classification performance. In other words, we obtained a slightly higher TPR (108/264 : 40.04%) this time. Again, its performance is below par on the class we are interested in.

We show confusion matrix of classification results obtained with BERT in Figure 5. We see from Figure 5 that performance of BERT is much worse than that of RF and SVM.

Our dataset is a mixture of different types of posts including personal information, opinions, events, information about articles and publications on human rights. Moreover, this is a class-imbalanced data set (10% of Tweets were based on factual Tweets about human right violation). We manually looked at the Tweets of both classes. We observed that a number of Tweets of majority class seems to be factual Tweets at first glance. However, they were either instructive texts or expressions about opinion on human rights. As an example, we show a Tweet that belong to the majority class (class '0'): "*Students have the right to protest. Violence against peacefully protesting students —or anywhere else—can't be justified under any circumstances. As protests spread to campuses, we urge authorities to respect the right to dissent by peaceful protesters*". It is an opinion and not a factual post. It has a negative polarity. However, it does not express the fact that any harm was caused or any human right was violated. Such type of Tweets of training data could be one the reasons for poor TPR. We conjecture that another reason for poor TPR is the nature of our gold-standard dataset, which is class-imbalanced. Investigating this area (i.e. dealing with class-imbalanced data) is part of our future research plans.

5. Conclusions and Future Work

In this work, we investigated detection of violation of human rights via social media. We chose one of the most popular micro-blogging websites, Twitter, for our investigation. We used supervised learning algorithms in order to build human rights violation identification (HRVI) models such as Random Forest, Support Vector Machine, and state-of-the-art classification algorithm BERT. For this, we manually created a gold-standard dataset, which is in fact one of the main contributions of this work. The performance of our classifiers seem to be excellent in this task if we consider both classes. However, their performance are below par on positive class (i.e. on identifying Tweets in relation to incidents of human right violation). We identified a number of potential causes for this disparity. In order to counter this anomaly, in future, we plan to examine the fol-

[9] `https://scikit-learn.org/`

[10] `https://scikit-learn.org/stable/`

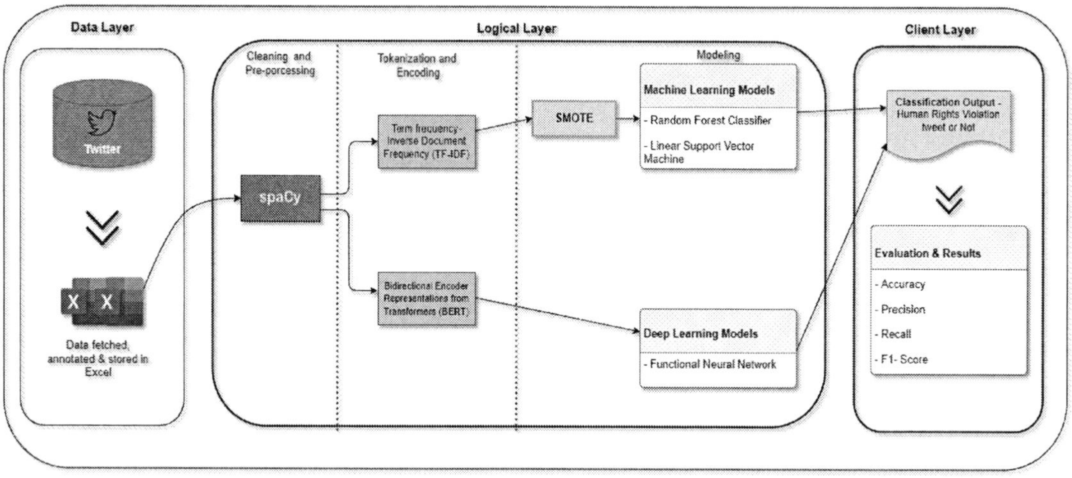

Figure 2: Project Architecture

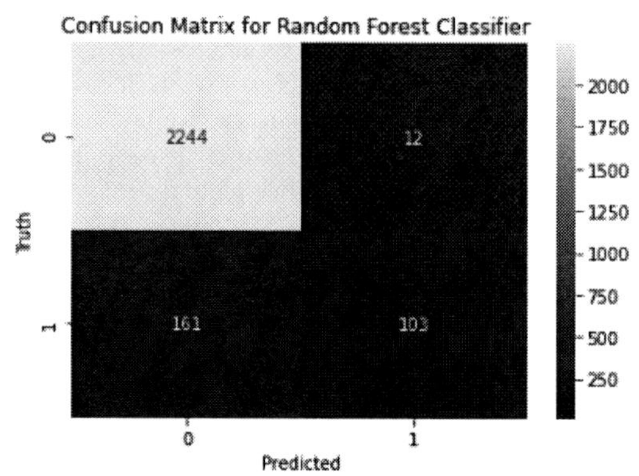

Figure 3: Confusion Matrix: RF

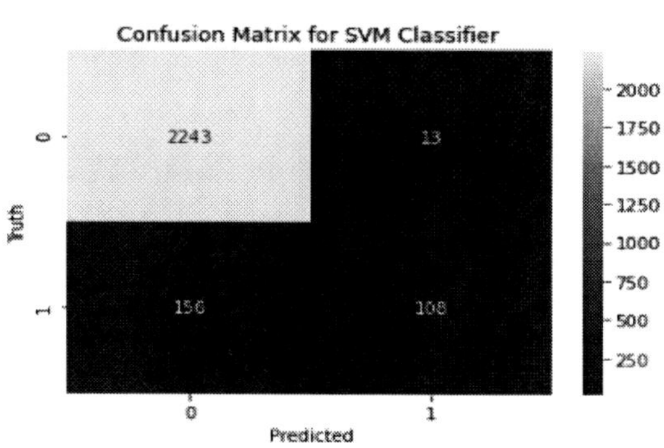

Figure 4: Confusion Matrix: SVM

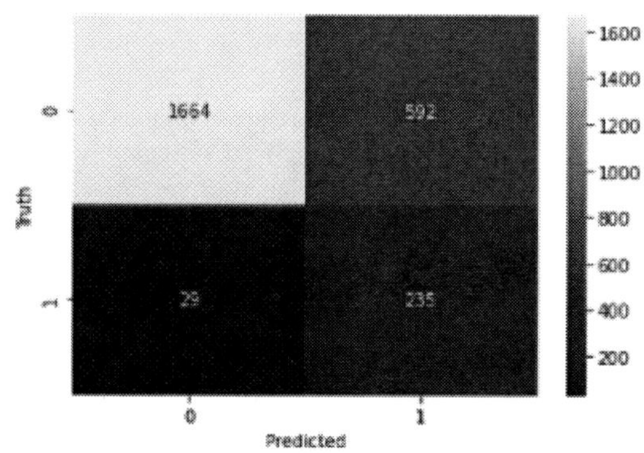

Figure 5: Confusion Matrix: BERT

lowing aspects of the task: (i) we want to increase the coverage for the positive class, (ii) exploring state-of-the-art strategies that deal with class-imbalanced text data, and (iii) play with different hyperparameters of the BERT model.

Acknowledgement

A part of this research was conducted with the financial support of the Horizon 2020 project ITFLOWS under Grant Agreement No. 882986 and the ADAPT SFI Research Centre at Munster Technological University. The ADAPT SFI Centre for Digital Media Technology is funded by Science Foundation Ireland through the SFI Research Centres Programme and is co-funded under the European Regional Development Fund (ERDF) through Grant 13/RC/2106.

6. Bibliographical References

Alhelbawy, A., Lattimer, M., Kruschwitz, U., Fox, C., and Poesio, M. (2020). An nlp-powered human rights monitoring platform. *Expert Systems with Applications*, 153:113365.

Davidson, T., Warmsley, D., Macy, M., and Weber, I. (2017). Automated hate speech detection and the problem of offensive language.

Devlin, J., Chang, M.-W., Lee, K., and Toutanova, K. (2018a). Bert: Pre-training of deep bidirectional transformers for language understanding. *arXiv preprint arXiv:1810.04805*.

Devlin, J., Chang, M., Lee, K., and Toutanova, K. (2018b). BERT: pre-training of deep bidirectional transformers for language understanding. *CoRR*, abs/1810.04805.

Fitri, V. A., Andreswari, R., and Hasibuan, M. A. (2019). Sentiment analysis of social media twitter with case of anti-lgbt campaign in indonesia using naïve bayes, decision tree, and random forest algorithm. *Procedia Computer Science*, 161:765–772. The Fifth Information Systems International Conference, 23-24 July 2019, Surabaya, Indonesia.

Fleiss, J. L. and Cohen, J. (1973). The equivalence of weighted kappa and the intraclass correlation coefficient as measures of reliability. *Educational and Psychological Measurement*, 33(3):613–619.

Hamdan, H., Bellot, P., and Bechet, F. (2015). Lsislif: Feature extraction and label weighting for sentiment analysis in twitter. In *Proceedings of the 9th International Workshop on Semantic Evaluation (SemEval 2015)*. Association for Computational Linguistics.

Haque, R., Ramadurai, A., Hasanuzzaman, M., and Way, A. (2019). Mining purchase intent in twitter. In *Proceedings of CICLing 2019, the 20th International Conference on Computational Linguistics and Intelligent Text Processing*, La Rochelle, France.

Jiang, D., Luo, X., Xuan, J., and Xu, Z. (2017). Sentiment computing for the news event based on the social media big data. *IEEE Access*, 5:2373–2382.

Kanakaraddi, S. G., Chikaraddi, A. K., Gull, K. C., and Hiremath, P. S. (2020). Comparison study of sentiment analysis of tweets using various machine learning algorithms. In *2020 International Conference on Inventive Computation Technologies (ICICT)*, pages 287–292.

Laskar, R. H. and Sunny, S. (2021). Indian journalist killed in line of duty by taliban. *The Hindustan Times*, Jul.

Lim, Y. Q., Lim, C. M., Gan, K. H., and Samsudin, N. H. (2020). Text sentiment analysis on twitter to identify positive or negative context in addressing inept regulations on social media platform. In *2020 IEEE 10th Symposium on Computer Applications Industrial Electronics (ISCAIE)*, pages 96–101.

Mikolov, T., Chen, K., Corrado, G., and Dean, J. (2013). Efficient estimation of word representations in vector space. *arXiv preprint arXiv:1301.3781*.

Neethu, M. S. and Rajasree, R. (2013). Sentiment analysis in twitter using machine learning techniques. In *2013 Fourth International Conference on Computing, Communications and Networking Technologies (ICCCNT)*, pages 1–5.

Qin, Q., Hu, W., and Liu, B. (2020). Feature projection for improved text classification. In *Proceedings of the 58th Annual Meeting of the Association for Computational Linguistics*, pages 8161–8171, Online, July. Association for Computational Linguistics.

Singh, R. P., Haque, R., Hasanuzzaman, M., and Way, A. (2020a). Identifying complaints from product reviews: A case study on hindi. In *Proceedings of the Irish Conference on Artificial Intelligence and Cognitive Science (AICS 2020)*, Dublin, Ireland.

Singh, R. P., Haque, R., Hasanuzzaman, M., and Way, A. (2020b). Identifying complaints from product reviews in low-resource scenarios via neural machine translation. In *Proceedings of ICON 2020: 17th International Conference on Natural Language Processing*, Patna, India.

Somula, R., Dinesh Kumar, K., Aravindharamanan, S., and Govinda, K. (2020). Twitter sentiment analysis based on us presidential election 2016. In Suresh Chandra Satapathy, et al., editors, *Smart Intelligent Computing and Applications*, pages 363–373, Singapore. Springer Singapore.

Vaswani, A., Shazeer, N., Parmar, N., Uszkoreit, J., Jones, L., Gomez, A. N., Kaiser, L., and Polosukhin, I. (2017). Attention is all you need. *CoRR*, abs/1706.03762.

Waseem, Z. and Hovy, D. (2016). Hateful symbols or hateful people? predictive features for hate speech detection on Twitter. In *Proceedings of the NAACL Student Research Workshop*, pages 88–93, San Diego, California, June. Association for Computational Linguistics.

Williams, E., Rodrigues, P., and Novak, V. (2020). Accenture at checkthat! 2020: If you say so: Post-hoc fact-checking of claims using transformer-based models. *arXiv preprint arXiv:2009.02431*.

Zahoor, S. and Rohilla, R. (2020). Twitter sentiment analysis using lexical or rule based approach: A case study. In *2020 8th International Conference on Reliability, Infocom Technologies and Optimization (Trends and Future Directions) (ICRITO)*, pages 537–542.

Proceedings of CSR-NLP I @LREC 2022, pages 46–51
Marseille, 25 June 2022

Inclusion in CSR Reports: The Lens from a Data-driven Machine Learning Model

Lu Lu, Jinghang Gu, Chu-Ren Huang
Hong Kong Polytechnic University
lulubfsu@gmail.com, {jinghang.gu, churen.huang}@polyu.edu.hk

Abstract

Inclusion, as one of the foundations in the diversity, equity, and inclusion initiative, concerns the degree of being treated as an ingroup member in a workplace. Despite of its importance in a corporate's ecosystem, the inclusion strategies and its performance are not adequately addressed in corporate social responsibility (CSR) and CSR reporting. This study proposes a machine learning and big data-based model to examine inclusion through the use of stereotype content in actual language use. The distribution of the stereotype content in general corpora of a given society is utilized as a baseline, with which texts from a corporate under discussion are compared. This study not only propose a model to identify and classify inclusion in language use, but also provides insights to measure and track progress by including inclusion in CSR reports and to build an inclusive corporate team.

Keywords: corporate social responsibility (CSR) reports, inclusion, word embeddings, baseline, big data

1. Introduction

Diversity, equity and inclusion (DE&I) are essential cornerstones of Corporate Social Responsibility (CSR) (Fenwick and Bierema, 2008; Grosser and Moon, 2005). The CSR report, as one of the most important outlets to communicate a corporate's social engagement and impact, provides insights to a corporate's social norms. However, DE&I, especially the inclusion, lacks adequate attention in CSR reports (Hunt et al., 2020, among many others). As inclusion focuses on treating a person as 'we' (ingroup) rather than 'them' (outgroup), and is mediated by the use of stereotyping languages, we are interested to examine inclusion through Warmth and Competence, the two universal dimensions in stereotype content (Fiske et al., 2002). This niche in CSR reporting motivates us to employ machine learning techniques and big data samples to study stereotype content in actual language use. Word embedding, as a powerful technique in studying the semantic association between words, are employed to identify the stereotype content and analyze its distribution in a general corpus and use the results as a baseline. Furthermore, the collection of internal and external documents and texts in a corporate can be utilized to measure and compare with the baseline, hence developing a better understanding of the progress of a corporate's efforts in promoting inclusion. This study aims to establish and demonstrate a model that can be applied to CSRs in the future in order to unveil the corporate's stand on inclusion and their DE&I efforts at large. Measuring a corporate's use of stereotype content against the society's norm of stereotypes in general corpora, this study gives CSR reports a clear baseline to do better than.

The rest of the paper is organized as follows. Section 2 reviews the previous studies regarding inclusion, stereotypes, CSR reports and machine learning approaches. In Section 3, a word embedding based model to study stereotype content in general corpora (i.e. baseline) and the corporate corpus is proposed and referred to as the Word Embedding Inclusion Model (WEIM). We then, in Section 4, report a research plan to examine the distribution of Warmth and Competence of different temporal points in the US society from American English corpora and use the findings as a baseline, which can be compared with corporate datasets. The paper is concluded in Section 5.

2. Literature review

2.1 Diversity, Equity and Inclusion in Businesses

Social responsibility, also known as corporate social responsibility, refers to the ways that a corporate positions itself to make positive influence on the community and society at large (Fenwick and Bierema, 2008). CSR initiatives require a corporate not only to focus on making money and profitable gains, but also take a longer and strategic view of their 'impact economically, socially, environmentally, and in terms of human rights', on a wide range of stakeholders (CIPD, 2003). CSR is an important approach to align business strategies with the value and well-being of the society, thus strengthening the connection between employers and employees. CSR initiatives have been incorporated into the branding of the corporate (Hon and Gamor, 2021).

While CSR relating to personal well-being starts from inside the corporate, it is communicated externally through outlets, such as corporate websites, blogs, and public reports showing their businesses' cultures and priorities. One of the most important public-facing reporting outlets is the CSR reports, providing insights into an organization's workplace norms, hiring practices, and overarching aspects of organizational culture (De Stefano et al., 2018).

DE&I initiatives, aiming to create a welcoming environment for less privileged identities, are an essential aspect in employers' CSR strategies, due to social pressure, increased diversity in clients, and public policies (Moore et al., 2017). Grosser and Moon (2005), for example, report the criteria and benefits of including gender equality into CSR reports. The 2020 analyst report by McKinsey & Company shows that the gap in ethnic diversity is larger than gender diversity between the top-quartile and the fourth quartile corporates, and this trend is likely to continue (Hunt et al., 2020). The lack of ethnic minority diversity is even more evident in the UK and US. The representation of ethnic minorities in the executive team in the UK and US is 13 percent in 2019, which only increased from 7 percent in 2014, whereas the global dataset shows that 14 percent of ethnic minorities are represented in the executive team, increased from 12 percent in 2017. Even though DE&I is the crucial aspect of marketing and talent acquisition, inclusion, which is the 'degree to which an employee is accepted and treated as an insider by others in a work system' (Pelled et al., 1999), is not yet prioritized in corporates' CSR reporting and strategies. In the tourism workforce, for example, Hon and Gamor (2021) have advocated for the inclusion of minority groups as CSR strategies and corporate images. Furthermore, in the advancement of DE&I culture in industrial settings, employees' negative sentiments towards inclusion in their workplace experience is markedly worse than the ones towards diversity in McKinsey's diversity report in 2020 (Hunt et al., 2020). This challenge is still visible for relatively diverse corporates. Among many aspects of inclusion, freedom from bias and discrimination is one of the important factors.

As businesses face increased demands for inclusion, it is worth continued research to help corporates identify their advantages and problems compared with the norm in the society, and thus, based on that, corporates can further enhance inclusive practices, organizational cultures, and policies.

2.2 Inclusion, Stereotypes, and Language Use

Inclusion can be affected by negative attitudes and stereotypes (Sanders and Sullivan, 2010; Krischler et al., 2018). Being both positive and negative, stereotypes in both polarities can be found in a given social group. In Stereotype Content Model (SCM), Warmth and Competence are two universal dimensions to evaluate stereotype content (Fiske et al., 2002; Fiske, 2018). Warmth (trustworthiness, sociability) can be depicted as 'good-hearted' and 'benevolent', and features such as 'competent', 'intelligent' are used to describe Competence (capable, agentic). The degree that Warmth and Competence are ascribed to high and low levels reflects how 'we' believe and evaluate 'others'. The arrays of Warmth and Competence are further classified based on their high and low levels: High Warmth (HW), Low Warmth (LW), High Competence (HC), and Low Competence (LC). The combined interpretation of the stereotype content and its levels define different social groups: for instance, elderly people are regarded as HW-LC, Whites are HW-HC, the rich are commonly believed as LW-HC, and Blacks as LH-LC (Fiske et al., 2002, Durante et al., 2017a, 2017b). According to the SCM, a society's default group or ingroup is believed to be 'us' that are high on both Warmth and Competence, whereas the group of 'them', depicting a stereotype of exclusion, is low on both dimensions. The rest of the combinations are ambivalent, meaning that they are high on one dimension only, such as being high in Warmth but low in Competence (Durante et al., 2017b).

There have been several attempts to apply the SCM to investigate the actual use of languages. In Dupree and Fiske's (2019) study, they apply the SCM to analyze the past campaign speeches of the White Republican and Democratic presidential candidates and compared their speeches with different target audiences. The findings exhibit that, when addressing audiences who are mostly minority groups, Democrats use more Warmth than Competence. As the use of stereotype is reflective of social inclusion, analyzing the distribution along the Warmth and Competence dimensions in actual language use can reveal inclusion towards a group in a natural way.

2.3 Word Embedding in Stereotypes

The study of stereotypes has been broadly explored with human subject research (Katz and Braly, 1933; Fiske et al., 2002) and text-based analysis (Henley, 1989). Recent development in machine learning offers great promise and valuable insights to understand stereotypes. Word embeddings are an unsupervised neural network-based technique to capture semantic associations of words with relationships between vectors. Word2vec (Mikolov et al., 2013a, 2013b), as one of the most popular techniques in word embeddings, takes a large amount of textual data as input and represents a word as a list of low-dimension vectors. The cosine similarity function between the vectors indicates the degree of semantic similarities between the words. For example, a higher cosine similarity score can be found between words 'man' and 'woman' than the pair of 'man' and 'pen'. The vector representation can be obtained by the models of Skip-gram and Common Bag of Words. This project will choose the Skip-gram model as we are more interested in predicting a word within a certain range before and after the target word in the same sentence (a.k.a. window size).

There have been some studies using word embedding techniques to study stereotype languages. Garg et al.

(2018) have proved that word embeddings are robust in extracting and analyzing ethnic and gender stereotypes over 100 years. Since Garg et al.'s (2018) longitudinal survey, word embeddings have been widely applied as a method of extracting features out of texts and using those features as an input to machine learning model to shed light on stereotype expressions and the attitudes towards them (Charlesworth et al., 2021; Kroon et al., 2021). However, there has been less work on applying machine learning techniques to examine the SCM and analyze how the properties of stereotype content are manifested in actual languages.

Given the fact that little research exists about how inclusion is addressed in CSR reports with machine learning tools, this study attempts to address this niche by using word embedding techniques to analyze stereotype content. Specifically, the distribution of stereotype content in a general corpus will be employed as a baseline, with which the one in corporate corpora, consisting of published resources of a corporate, will be compared and reported in CSR reports. In the rest of the study, we will detail the model based on word embedding techniques on stereotype content with a preliminary case study.

3. Methodology

In this section, the Word Embedding-based Inclusion Model (WEIM) in CSR reports is proposed to address the niche on inclusion as reflected in the language use of stereotype content. Figure 1 illustrates the architecture of the proposed method, which is a machine learning framework that classifies stereotypes into Warmth and Competence, and identifies the keywords associated with the two categories based on deep semantic representation.

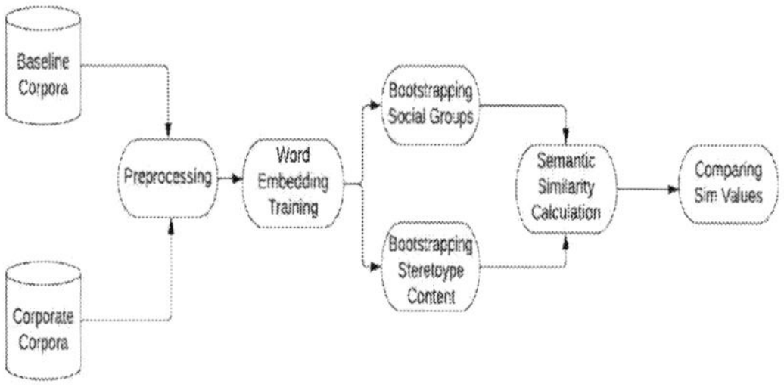

Figure 1: The pipeline of the Word Embedding-based Inclusion Model (WEIM).

In this model, the baseline corpus and the corporate corpus, respectively, go through the pipeline in the WEIM. The unstructured raw texts in each corpus, after preprocessing, was trained on word embeddings, which converts each word into a vector for calculation. In the following bootstrapping module, keywords about particular social groups (e.g. ethnic groups, gender groups) and stereotype content of Warmth and Competence were automatically extracted from each corpus. For example, in a case study on ethnic groups in the USA, 'Asians', 'Blacks', 'Hispanics', and 'Whites' can be used as seed words to extract the 150 most similar words to those seed words for each ethnic group. In a similar way, seed words related to the positive and negative Warmth and Competence were chosen to automatically extract the 150 most similar words based on the Euclidian distance. After manual checking, the remaining words are the valid keywords used in the rest of the analysis. In the next module on the semantic similarity calculation, the keywords in each social group and in each positive/negative category of the two stereotype content dimensions were iterated and paired to calculate the average cosine similarity score of that particular social group in terms of its stereotype content. Specifically, for each corpus, we calculate the cosine similarity score of the keywords pairing between each social group and each component in the stereotype content. We have until now collected the average sim values of positive and negative Competence and positive/negative Warmth that pair with a given social group, in terms of the corporate corpus data and the baseline corpus data. Finally, we can compare the two sets of data and examine the performance of the language of inclusion in corporate data vis-à-vis the baseline general corpus data.

4. A Proposal for a Study on Ethnic Inclusion

In this section, we will use a set of American English corpora in general to illustrate how we can incorporate the data generated from this baseline corpus to better understand the use of stereotype in corporates. The baseline corpora for this case study are the Brown Family Corpora, consisting of a) the original Brown corpus (Francis and Kucera, 1979), b) the Freiburg update of the Brown corpus (Frown; Hundt et al., 1999), and c) the recent update of the Brown corpus around the year 2009 (Crown; Xu and Liang, 2009). These three corpora of American English follow the same sampling pattern in the Brown corpus. Each of the three corpus contains 500 documents with approximately 2,000 words on average, consisting of textual collections published in the years 1961, 1991, and 2009 (± 1 year), respectively. The three corpora cover four broad text types: press, general prose, learned writing, and fiction, which is meant to present American language use in general. In total, the baseline corpora have approximately three million words and contain three temporal points in the 1960s, 1990s, to approximately the 2010s. Additionally, the corporate corpus can be composed of internal and external documents and texts published by a given corporate, such as news reports about this corporate, past public-facing reports (e.g., CSR reports), corporate websites, blogs, and transcripts of recorded meetings in internal and external channels (with prior ethical approval). Both baseline corpora and the corporate corpora will undergo the same pipelines as detailed in the rest of the section, including but not limited to following the same preprocessing methods and using the same seed words to extract social group and stereotype content wordlists. In what follows, I will propose a preliminary study to identify and extract information in the baseline corpus, and build on the data reported in Lu et al. (to be submitted) to examine the baseline vis-à-vis the corporate corpus.

In this preliminary study, following the WEIM model, we will use Python to preprocess raw data from corpora, such as turning all letters to lower cases, removing non-alphanumeric characters, before training word embeddings. Gensim's word2vec skip-gram model (Mikolov et al., 2013a) will be used and each word will be returned with 300 dimensions in our training corpus. Each corpus will be trained individually to examine the over-time variation of the three temporal points. Finally, some simple analogy tests (e.g. man is to king, as woman is to___) will be performed to warrant the quality of the embedding models.

In the next module of bootstrapping, we consider stereotypes in the four ethnic groups in the US, namely Whites, Blacks, Hispanics, and Asians (e.g., Durante et al., 2017a). After word embedding training, seed words of 'Whites', 'Blacks', 'Hispanics', and 'Asians' can be used to bootstrap ethnic groups in the corpus. According to their cosine similarity scores, the first 150 most similar words to those seed words can be automatically extracted as the wordlist for ethnic groups. As for high/low levels of Warmth and Competence, seed words of 'warm' and 'warmth' (+W), 'unkind' and 'unfriendly' (-W), 'competence' and 'competent' (+W), and 'incompetence' and 'incompetent' (-C) will be used as seed words to extract, for example, the top 100 words that are similar to those seed words. Manual checking will be performed to 1) keep positive words in the positive groups and negative words in the negative groups; 2) remove irrelevant words generated from the wordlists. The wordlists of stereotype content will be paired with ethnic groups (e.g. (Japanese, kind) and (Chinese, friendly)) to compute the cosine similarity scores.

For this preliminary proposal, a sub-corpus with corporate texts from the baseline will be extracted and used as the corporate corpus. Based on the metadata of Brown, Frown, and Crown corpora, texts, such as news reports, about corporates or industries will be extracted to build the corporate corpus. This corpus of raw texts will follow the same pipelines as the baseline corpus to get word embedding score of each word and the similarity scores of the pair of the ethnic group and stereotype content.

Lu et al. (manuscript) used the same three baseline corpora as this current study, and also followed the similar approach as detailed above. In their research, data show that Asians are always ascribed to LW and HC and Blacks to HW and LC, the stereotype of which are supported by many social psychological studies (e.g., Swencionis et al., 2017; Froehlich and Schulte 2019). Even though questionnaire-based studies (e.g. Fiske et al. 2002) show that high value of Competence and Warmth shows inclusion, Lu et al. (manuscript) argue that HW and HC may not necessarily be the indicators of inclusion in actual language use. In their data, they found that Asians do not use HW to represent their inclusion. Instead, the consistent pattern of LW and HC in Asians vis-à-vis the equally consistent pattern of HW and LC in Blacks, and the tendency that Asians are inclined to be grouped together with Hispanics and Whites imply that the (dis)association with a particular ethnic group is a special way to represent inclusion in the actual language use. The other finding that is worth our attention is that, while Blacks are usually assigned with high warmth category, this is not true in the Brown corpus, where Whites are assigned with high warmth. On the other hand, this unusual pattern may align with the white supremacy view in the 1960s when the Brown corpus were constructed.

Building upon their findings regarding the distribution of Warmth and Competence in the baseline corpus, we can compare the results generated from the corporate corpus. The practical application for this comparison in a CSR report can be captured threefold. Firstly, the baseline corpus presents the norm of stereotype use in a given society (USA in this case study) at different temporal points. For example, it is likely to see a surge of content in describing Whites are warmth in the 1960s' corporate data in the USA, whereas Blacks are increasingly perceived as being warm since 1990s. Secondly, the WEIM applies the same seed words to bootstrap and the same methodology to calculate, and thus compare the stereotype language use in corporate data versus the general social trend. For example, the high competence score of Asians does not necessarily imply that a corporate is inclusive in this aspect, because the high competence scores in Asians can be the baseline of a society in general. Thirdly, the WEIM encourages a balanced view of high and low stereotype content towards any given group of people, thus promoting inclusion in workplace and society.

5. Conclusion

This paper proposed the model of WEIM, a word embedding based approach to use general corpora as a baseline to better understand the stereotype content in corporate language dataset, thus promoting the inclusion in CSR reports, which rarely use machine learning techniques and big data samples. We then propose a preliminary case study to figure out the inclusion of ethnic minorities in the actual language use of American English in general corpus vis-à-vis the sub-corpus of corporate texts in three different temporal points. The results from general corpus data will be treated as a baseline to help corporates further measure and compare the distribution of stereotype content in corporate datasets, and, eventually, promote the incorporation of inclusion in CSR reports.

References

Charlesworth T. E. S., Yang V., Mann T. C., Kurdi B., & Banaji M. R. (2021). Gender Stereotypes in Natural Language: Word Embeddings Show Robust Consistency Across Child and Adult Language Corpora of More Than 65 Million Words. *Psychological Science. 32*(2):218–240.

CIPD (2003), *Corporate Social Responsibility and HR's Role.* Chartered Institute of Personnel and Development, London.

De Stefano, F., Bagdadli, S., & Camuffo, A. (2018). The HR role in corporate social responsibility and sustainability: A boundary-shifting literature review. *Human Resource Management, 57*(2), 549-566.

Dupree, C. H., & Fiske, S. T. (2019). Self-presentation in interracial settings: The competence downshift by White liberals. *Journal of Personality and Social Psychology, 117*(3), 579–604.

Durante, F., Fiske, S. T., Gelfand, M. J., Crippa, F., Suttora, C., Stillwell, A., ... & Teymoori, A. (2017a). Ambivalent stereotypes link to peace, conflict, and inequality across 38 nations. *Proceedings of the National Academy of Sciences, 114*(4), 669–674.

Durante, F., Tablante, C. B., & Fiske, S. T. (2017b). Poor but warm, rich but cold (and competent): Social classes in the stereotype content model. *Journal of Social Issues, 73*(1), 138–157.

Fenwick, T., & Bierema, L. (2008). Corporate social responsibility: issues for human resource development professionals. *International Journal of training and Development, 12*(1), 24-35.

Fiske, S. T. (2018). Stereotype content: Warmth and competence endure. *Current directions in psychological science, 27*(2), 67–73.

Fiske, S. T., Cuddy, A. J., Glick, P., & Xu, J. (2002). A model of (often mixed) stereotype content: competence and warmth respectively follow from perceived status and competition. *Journal of personality and social psychology, 82*(6), 878–902.

Francis, W. N., & Kucera, H. (1979). Brown corpus manual. *Letters to the Editor, 5*(2), 7.

Froehlich, L., & Schulte, I. (2019). Warmth and competence stereotypes about immigrant groups in Germany. *PLoS ONE, 14*(9), e0223103.

Garg, N., Schiebinger, L., Jurafsky, D., & Zou, J. (2018). Word embeddings quantify 100 years of gender and ethnic stereotypes. *Proceedings of the National Academy of Sciences, 115*(16), E3635–E3644.

Grosser, K., & Moon, J. (2005). Gender mainstreaming and corporate social responsibility: Reporting workplace issues. *Journal of business ethics, 62*(4), 327-340.

Henley N. M. (1989). Molehill or mountain? What we know and don't know about sex bias in language. In Crawford M. and Gentry M. (eds.) *Gender and Thought: Psychological Perspectives.* New York: Springer. pp 59–78.

Hon, A. H., & Gamor, E. (2021). The inclusion of minority groups in tourism workforce: Proposition of an impression management framework through the lens of corporate social responsibility. *International Journal of Tourism Research.*

Hope Pelled, L., Ledford, Jr, G. E., & Albers Mohrman, S. (1999). Demographic dissimilarity and workplace inclusion. *Journal of Management studies, 36*(7), 1013-1031.

Hundt, M., A. Sand, and P. Skandera. (1999). *Manual of Information to accompany The Freiburg – Brown Corpus of American English ('Frown').* Freiburg: Department of English. Albert-Ludwigs-Universität Freiburg. http://khnt.aksis.uib.no/icame/manuals/frown/INDEX.HTM.

Hunt, V., Prince, S., Dixon-Fyle, S., & Dolan, K. (2020). *Diversity wins: How inclusion matters.* McKinsey & Company.

Katz D., Braly K. (1933). Racial stereotypes of one hundred college students. *J Abnorm Soc Psychol* 28:280–290.

Krischler, M., Pit-ten Cate, I. M., & Krolak-Schwerdt, S. (2018). Mixed stereotype content and attitudes toward students with special educational needs and their inclusion in regular schools in Luxembourg. *Research in Developmental Disabilities, 75*, 59-67.

Kroon, A. C., Trilling, D., & Raats, T. (2021). Guilty by association: Using word embeddings to measure ethnic stereotypes in news coverage. *Journalism & Mass Communication Quarterly, 98*(2), 451–477.

Lu, L., Gu, J., & Huang, C.-R. (manuscript). Warmth and Competence of ethnic stereotypes in American English: A data-driven machine learning approach.

Mikolov, T., Corrado, G., Chen, K., & Dean, J. (2013a). Efficient estimation of word representations in vector space. In ICLR:, *Proceeding of the International Conference on Learning Representations Workshop Track* (pp. 1301–3781).

Mikolov, T., Sutskever, I., Chen, K., Corrado, G. S., & Dean, J. (2013b). Distributed representations of words and phrases and their compositionality. *Advances in neural information processing systems*, 26.

Moore, K., McDonald, P., & Bartlett, J. (2017). The social legitimacy of disability inclusive human resource practices: the case of a large retail organisation. *Human Resource Management Journal*, *27*(4), 514-529.

Sanders, M. S., & Sullivan, J. M. (2010). Category inclusion and exclusion in perceptions of African Americans: Using the stereotype content model to examine perceptions of groups and individuals. *Race, Gender & Class*, 201-222.

Schnabel, T., Labutov, I., Mimno, D., & Joachims, T. (2015, September). Evaluation methods for unsupervised word embeddings. In *Proceedings of the 2015 conference on empirical methods in natural language processing* (pp. 298–307).

Swencionis, J. K., & Fiske, S. T. (2016). Promote up, ingratiate down: Status comparisons drive warmth-competence tradeoffs in impression management. *Journal of Experimental Social Psychology*, *64*, 27–34.

Xu, Jiajin & Maocheng Liang. (2013). A tale of two C's: Comparing English varieties with Crown and CLOB. *ICAME Journal*37: 175-183.

Proceedings of CSR-NLP I @LREC 2022, pages 52–57
Marseille, 25 June 2022

Towards Classification of Legal Pharmaceutical Text using GAN-BERT

Tapan Auti[1], Rajdeep Sarkar[1], Bernardo Stearns[1], Atul Kr. Ojha[1], Arindam Paul[2], Michaela Comerford[2], Jay Megaro[2], John Mariano[2], Vall Herard[2], John P. McCrae[1]
[1] Data Science Institute, National University of Ireland Galway, Ireland, [2] FMR LLC, Boston, USA
{tapan.auti, rajdeep.sarkar, bernardo.stearns, atulkumar.ojha, john.mccrae}@insight-centre.org
{arindam.paul, michaela.comerford, jay.megaro, john.mariano, vall.herard}@fmr.com

Abstract

Pharmaceutical text classification is an important area of research for commercial and research institutions working in the pharmaceutical domain. Addressing this task is challenging due to the need of expert verified labelled data which can be expensive and time consuming to obtain. Towards this end, we leverage predictive coding methods for the task as they have been shown to generalise well for sentence classification. Specifically, we utilise GAN-BERT architecture to classify pharmaceutical texts. To capture the domain specificity, we propose to utilise the BioBERT model as our BERT model in the GAN-BERT framework. We conduct extensive evaluation to show the efficacy of our approach over baselines on multiple metrics.

Keywords: Generative Adversarial Network, Text classification, BERT

1. Introduction

Occurrence frequency of misleading statements has increased in industries such as financial, legal, social media, health, biomedical and pharmaceutical. Meanwhile natural language processing has grown rapidly in particular due to machine learning and deep learning methods that provide mechanisms to classify text automatically. Various innovative approaches have been proposed. Devlin et al. (2019) proposed a BERT (Devlin et al., 2019) based classifier for the classification problem. Jofche et al. (2021) suggested the use of transfer learning for knowledge extraction from the classified pharmaceutical text while Croce et al. (2020) proposed a Generative Adversarial Network (GAN) based model leveraging the BERT architecture for the text classification. Sarkar et al. (2021) investigated Naive-Bayes, SVM, Multi-Layer Perceptron (MLP), Sentence-BERT(S-BERT), Laser, Zero-Shot and Few-Shot approaches to legal-financial text classification.

In the United States, the Food and Drug Administration (FDA) is responsible for protecting public health by ensuring the safety, efficacy of drugs. Promotional communications must meet the following criteria, which are based upon the FDCA: be clear, accurate and truthful, not be misleading, promote only cleared or approved intended use, be supported by valid scientific evidence, and include a fair balance between benefits and risks. In this paper, we focus on classification in the pharmaceutical industry for detecting misleading claims. We have adopted and extended a triplet network classifier (Sarkar et al., 2021) and GAN-BERT. Both models are relatively unexplored in the pharmaceutical domain. Firstly, we train a system on Naive-Bayes, SVM, MLP, S-BERT (Reimers and Gurevych, 2019) and Laser (Artetxe and Schwenk, 2019). Secondly, we train a system on GAN-BERT. Finally, to factor the domain specificity, we replace the BERT of GAN-BERT architecture with BioBERT (Lee et al., 2020), which is a BERT architecture fine-tuned on biomedical text. The semi-supervised approach of GAN-BioBERT with GAN's generative nature and the results of Bio-BERT on biomedical datasets motivated us to use them to optimise our results.

2. Related Work

Application of innovative techniques such as GAN-BERT, BERT, few-shot and zero-shot learning in the biomedical domain has been successfully explored. However, the extraction classification of biomedical and pharmaceutical text is difficult due to the domain specificity of terms and the inter-dependency of such terms with other tokens in the text. In most cases, it involves training models on large volumes of labelled data that can be expensive and time-consuming. Towards this end, Flores et al. (2019) posited FREGEX to extract biomedical features using regular expression. The authors used string based algorithms for extracting tokens having similar patterns and contextual features. Similarly, Flores et al. (2020) proposed CREGEX, an innovative method for automatically generating informative and discriminative regular expression.

With the advent of deep-learning based models, Yao et al. (2019) proposed a knowledge guided convolutional neural network model utilising a rule-based feature extractor for clinical text classification. Du et al. (2019) suggested the use of a label prediction network for biomedical text classification. On the other hand, Wu et al. (2021) proposed Bio-IE, a novel method utilising a hybrid neural network for extracting relations from biomedical text. They used multi-head enhanced convolutional graph to capture the complex relations and context information resisting noise. Luo (2017) proposed a LSTM model for learning word and contextual embeddings without the need of manual feature engineering.

Vaswani et al. (2017) posited transformer architecture for improving the representational capacity of LSTMs. Devlin et al. (2019) utilised the transformer architecture and proposed BERT to obtain contextualised representation of sentences as well as tokens in sentences. They showed the efficacy of BERT on various natural language processing tasks. Bio-BERT (Lee et al., 2020) is fine-tuned BERT which is pre-trained with bio-medical dataset for capturing the dependencies between domain specific terms.

Even though GAN-BERT gave good results on classification tasks, BERT's capacity to handle bio-medical data wasn't that great as it cannot extract those features. Due to this GAN-BERT failed on bio-medical dataset.

3. Methodology

In this section, we begin with a formal definition of the GAN architecture. We then outline the semi-supervised training of the GAN for legal pharmaceutical text classification. We begin by describing the semi-supervised training of GAN for text classification and then focus on the details of the Model Architecture used in this work.

3.1. Generative Adversarial Network

We leverage the GAN architecture for the classification task. The GAN architecture consists of two networks interacting with each other, a discriminator and a generator. The generator constructs 'fake' examples to deceive the discriminator during the classification task, while the discriminator is trained to distinguish the generated samples from the real samples present in the dataset. The generator and the discriminator are trained together in an adversarial setting. In this work, the GAN network is trained using the Minimax loss (Goodfellow et al., 2014) as outlined in Equation 1.

$$\mathcal{L} = \underset{G}{min}\,\underset{D}{max} (\mathbb{E}_{x \sim \mathbb{P}_{data}}[log(D(x))] + \mathbb{E}_{z \sim \mathbb{P}_z}[1 - log(D(G(z)))]) \quad (1)$$

where *D* and *G* are the discriminator and the generator network to be learned and z is the noise induced in the model to generate artificial samples using the generator.

3.2. Semi Supervised Training of Generative Adversarial Network

The goal of the classification task is to classify a sentence into one of *K* classes. Following Croce et al. (2020), we train the GAN in a semi-supervised setting, wherein the discriminator and the generator are trained together. Given a set of *K* classes for text classification, the discriminator is trained to classify a piece of text into one-of-*K* classes. In addition to the *K* classes, we add an extra *K+1* class to train the discriminator to classify the samples generated from the generator into the $K + 1^{th}$ class. Introducing the additional class enables the network to learn from unlabelled examples as well.

3.3. Model Architecture

We leverage the GAN-BERT architecture to classify legal pharmaceutical text in a semi-supervised setting. Given a text sequence $s = (w_1, w_2, ..., w_n)$ consisting of n tokens, we leverage a pre-trained BERT model to obtain a contextual representation of s. The BERT model encodes each token to a $d_{real} \in \mathbb{R}$ dimensional contextualised vector. We consider the CLS token representation of the BERT model as the representation of s. Mathematically we define it as:

$$\mathbf{e} = \text{BERT}(s_{data}) \quad (2)$$

$$\mathbf{s}_{data} = \mathbf{e}([CLS]) \quad (3)$$

where BERT denotes the BERT encoding architecture.

On the other hand, during semi-supervised training of the GAN, we sample a $d_{fake} \in \mathbb{R}$ vector as the noise vector for the generator. This noise vector is fed as input to the generator for generating adversarial examples. The generator then generates a $d_{real} \in \mathbb{R}$ dimensional vector which is then sent to the discriminator for classification. Mathematically, the generator network is defined as:

$$z \sim Uniform(0, 1) \quad (4)$$

$$\mathbf{s}_{G(z)} = MLP(z) \quad (5)$$

where the MLP is a 5 layer dense network with LeakyRelu activation function as the non-linearity in each layer. We do not introduce any activation function in the final layer of the MLP. The noise vector is sampled from a uniform distribution (0, 1).

Similar to the generator, the discriminator is also modelled as a multi-layer perceptron with 5 dense layers with LeakyRelu activation function in every layer except for the last layer. As the role of the discriminator is to classify the text into $K+1$ classes, the output from the final layer layer is passed through a Softmax layer to assign probabilities of the sentence belonging to a specific class. Mathematically we define the discriminator and the final classification as:

$$\text{logits} = MLP(\text{s}) \quad (6)$$

$$\text{P}_{class} = Softmax(\text{logits}) \quad (7)$$

where P_{class} denotes the probability of a text sequence belonging to a specific class.

For the final classification of a sentence, we utilise

Equation 8 to assign a class to the sentence.

$$\text{class}(s) = \begin{cases} \text{compliant} & p \geq \alpha \\ \text{non-compliant} & p < \alpha \end{cases} \quad (8)$$

where the threshold value α is a hyperparameter to be set.

4. Experimental Setup

In this section, we begin with a description of the dataset used in this work. Thereafter, we outline the baseline methods and the evaluation metrics on which we evaluate the performance of our proposed approach.

4.1. Dataset

We curated the dataset by considering external data sources concerning the pharmaceutical domain. This is a public dataset from Warning/Untitled letters from the FDA and FTC enforcements that was taken from the public data of largest pharmaceutical companies in the US. The dataset was then sent to a team of in-house experts for filtering low-quality instances. The resultant dataset contained 3,786 compliant sentences and 345 non-compliant sentences.

We split the final dataset into 70%, 15% and 15% as training, validation and test set. The resultant training set contained 2,784 and 245 compliant and non-compliant sentences respectively, while the validation and the test set contained 501 and 50 compliant and non-compliant sentences.

The Sentences being compliant and non-compliant is subject to the FDCA based on the information mentioned in them if any. Some examples from the dataset are mentioned in Table1.

4.2. Baseline and Evaluation Metrics

We compare our proposed approach again with the following baseline methods:

- Naive Bayes: We utilise the TF-IDF scores of tokens in the sentences to train a Naive Bayes model for the classification task.
- Multi-Layer Perceptron: We use the TF-IDF scores of tokens in the sentences as inputs to a 2-Layer dense neural network, with ReLu activation in the first layer, to train the classification model.
- SVM: Similar to the MLP model, we learn an SVM model for the classification task. We set the regularization parameter C and $gamma$ to 1.0 and 0.1 respectively.
- Sentence-Bert (Reimers and Gurevych, 2019): Sentence-BERT is Transformer (Vaswani et al., 2017) based sentence encoders that capture the rich semantic information in a sentence into a fixed-size vector. We encode each sentence using the Sentence-BERT architecture and then pass the sentence embedding to a 2 layer dense network for classification.
- LASER (Artetxe and Schwenk, 2019): Similar to the Sentence-BERT baseline, we encode each sentence using its LASER embedding and pass it to a 2 layer dense network for classification.

4.3. Implementation Details

For the Sentence-BERT baseline, we use the publicly available SBERT-BASE-NLI-MEAN-TOKENS [1] as our sentence encoder. While we utilise the LASER embeddings to encode the sentences to a 1024-dimensional vector. We use the publicly available BioBERT [2] as a replacement of the BERT model in our proposed approach.

We fine-tune the model with a learning rate of 5e-5 for both the generator and discriminator and batch size of 64 for 10 epochs with Adam optimizer. For the final classification, we plot the ROC curve and based on the distribution we set the α in Equation 8 to 0.7.

5. Results

In this section we outline the results of using our approach. We begin with the quantitative analysis of the performance of our approach against the baseline methods. Thereafter, we conduct an ablation study of replacing the Bio-BERT architecture with other BERT based encoders. Following this, we analyse the performance of our model in a few-shot setting wherein our approach and other baselines are supplied with a limited number of labelled examples. Finally, we conduct a qualitative analysis of the results and study a few cases where the labels assigned by our model is different from the gold-label. Analysis of our training suggests that, the training loss for generator and discriminator reduced with each epoch, and validation and test gave good results, which overruled the speculation of overfitting arising due to dataset being small to support deep learning models.

5.1. Quantitative Analysis

In this work, we propose a GAN based approach for pharmaceutical text classification. Table 2 outlines the performance of our proposed method against the different baseline methods used for the classification task. It can be observed that GAN-BioBERT achieves the best result amongst all models. It should be noted that GAN-BioBERT has a better performance than BioBERT showcasing the efficacy of our proposed approach.

5.2. Replacing BERT architecture

In our proposed approach, we replaced the BERT architecture in GAN-BERT with Bio-BERT model. To study the effectiveness of our choice of model, we replace the Bio-BERT model with BERT, RoBERTa and DistilBERT. We observe from Table 3 that the performance degrades when Bio-BERT is replaced with other

[1] https://huggingface.co/sentence-transformers/bert-base-nli-mean-tokens

[2] https://huggingface.co/dmis-lab/biobert-base-cased-v1.2

Table 1: Examples from our dataset to showcase the classes.

	Sentence	Model Label
1	FCS is a severe and rare disease caused by an enzyme deficiency that leads to the buildup of chylomicrons and a high risk of life-threatening pancreatitis.	compliant
2	We are committed to collaborating with the FDA to prevent or mitigate drug shortages that impact the health of patients.	compliant
3	Rosemary is one of the best essential oils that helps with headaches.	non-compliant
4	Tested and affordable Immune Plus Mouth Spray supports natural immune defense.	non-compliant

Table 2: Performance of our proposed method against different baseline methods for pharmaceutical text classification.

Model	Precision	Recall	F1	Accuracy
Naive Bayes	**1.00**	0.02	0.04	0.91
MLP	0.80	0.66	0.73	0.95
SVM	**1.00**	0.30	0.46	0.94
S-BERT	0.87	0.66	0.75	0.96
Laser	0	0	0	0.91
Bio-BERT	0.86	**0.86**	0.86	0.97
GAN-Bio-BERT	0.96	**0.86**	**0.91**	**0.98**

Table 3: Impact of the BERT architecture employed for the pharmaceutical text classification task.

Model	Precision	Recall	F1	Accuracy
GAN-BERT	0.81	0.84	0.82	0.97
GAN-RoBERTa	-	-	-	0.91
GAN-Bio-BERT	0.96	0.86	0.91	0.98

Table 4: Performance of our proposed approach against different baselines when a limited number of training examples are present. K denotes the number of training samples from each class used for training the models.

#Examples	Model	Precision	Recall	F1	Accuracy
K=10	BERT	**0.14**	0.26	0.18	0.78
	Bio-BERT	0.12	**0.58**	**0.20**	0.57
	GAN-Bio-BERT	0.00	0.00	0.00	**0.91**
K=20	BERT	0.11	0.16	0.13	0.80
	Bio-BERT	0.12	0.48	0.19	0.63
	GAN-Bio-BERT	**0.42**	**0.70**	**0.52**	**0.88**
K=50	BERT	0.13	0.54	0.21	0.63
	Bio-BERT	0.12	0.40	0.19	0.69
	GAN-Bio-BERT	**0.33**	**0.90**	**0.48**	**0.83**
K=100	BERT	0.17	0.74	0.28	0.65
	Bio-BERT	0.20	**0.86**	0.32	0.67
	GAN-Bio-BERT	**0.71**	0.68	**0.69**	**0.95**

BERT based models. This gives us a clear indication of the benefits of choosing a BERT model finetuned.

We observe from the Confusion Matrix of Figure 1 that the model misclassified only 9 out of the total 501 test examples and out of the 43 minority class examples only 2 were misclassfied. This clearly gives us the understanding that even after dataset being imbalanced the non-complaint class is aptly distinguished.

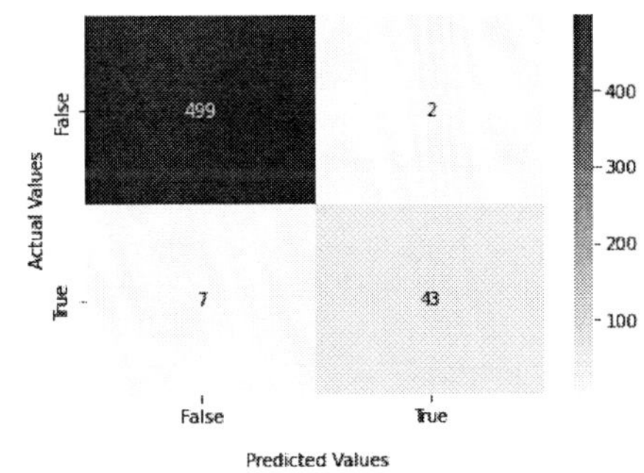

Figure 1: Confusion Matrix.

5.3. Few-Shot training

Getting labelled data can be time consuming and expensive. In this experiment, we train our proposed model with a limited number of labelled examples. We compare the performance of our proposed model again the BERT model and the Bio-BERT model.

Table 4 outlines the performance of different models when trained on a limited set of labelled data. It is interesting to notice that when there are only 10 labelled examples (K=10), GAN-Bio-BERT does not perform better than other baselines. This can be attributed to the generator generating poor quality samples, hence negatively impacting the performance of GAN-Bio-BERT. However, when the number of training samples (K) is increased, GAN-Bio-BERT outperforms different baselines by a large margin on the F1 score as well as Recall. This result demonstrates the efficacy of our proposed model on the classification task when a limited number of training examples are provided.

5.4. Qualitative Analysis

In this section, we analyse a few examples where the model assigns a different label to the sentence than the gold-label. Table 5 outlines four such cases. In the first and second examples, we can observe that the sen-

Table 5: Error Analysis: Examples where our proposed model produces classification labels different from the gold labels.

	Sentence	Model Result	Gold Label
1	Indulge in life's sweetest pleasures whenever you want.	compliant	non-compliant
2	Lower production of proinflammatory cytokines.	compliant	non-compliant
3	It is an anticholinergic medicine which helps the muscles around the airway in your lungs stay relaxed to prevent symptoms such as wheezing, cough, chest tightness, and shortness of breath.	non-compliant	compliant

tences are non-compliant but have been assigned the compliant class by the model. This might be due to the fact that these sentences seem incomplete, without more information it is difficult to say that they are non-compliant as they just state something without context. For the third sentence, we can observe that the sentences are compliant but have been assigned the non-compliant class by the model, this might be due to the context for both which implies that those specific medicines definitely work for the said symptoms, but it is extremely hard to know without having any knowledge about the medicines or context. This show that proper understanding of use cases of medicines and possible context about the sentences might help to correctly classify them.

6. Conclusion

In this work, we propose the use of predictive coding for the classification of pharmaceutical texts in the industry. We leverage the GAN-BioBERT architecture for the task and showcase its efficacy against different methods on multiple metrics. Additionally, we conduct a thorough ablation study to show the impact of our model of choice for the task.

7. Acknowledgements

This work has been funded by FMR LLC. Researchers at the Data Science Institute are supported by Science Foundation Ireland as part of Grant Number SFI/12/RC/2289_P2, Insight SFI Centre for Data Analytics.

8. Bibliographical References

Artetxe, M. and Schwenk, H. (2019). Massively multilingual sentence embeddings for zero-shot cross-lingual transfer and beyond. *Trans. Assoc. Comput. Linguistics*, 7:597–610.

Croce, D., Castellucci, G., and Basili, R. (2020). GAN-BERT: Generative adversarial learning for robust text classification with a bunch of labeled examples. In *Proceedings of the 58th Annual Meeting of the Association for Computational Linguistics*, pages 2114–2119, Online, July. Association for Computational Linguistics.

Devlin, J., Chang, M., Lee, K., and Toutanova, K. (2019). BERT: pre-training of deep bidirectional transformers for language understanding. In Jill Burstein, et al., editors, *Proceedings of the 2019 Conference of the North American Chapter of the Association for Computational Linguistics: Human Language Technologies, NAACL-HLT 2019, Minneapolis, MN, USA, June 2-7, 2019, Volume 1 (Long and Short Papers)*, pages 4171–4186. Association for Computational Linguistics.

Du, J., Chen, Q., Peng, Y., Xiang, Y., Tao, C., and Lu, Z. (2019). ML-Net: multi-label classification of biomedical texts with deep neural networks. *J. Am. Medical Informatics Assoc.*, 26(11):1279–1285.

Flores, C. A., Figueroa, R. L., and Pezoa, J. E. (2019). FREGEX: A feature extraction method for biomedical text classification using regular expressions. In *41st Annual International Conference of the IEEE Engineering in Medicine and Biology Society, EMBC 2019, Berlin, Germany, July 23-27, 2019*, pages 6085–6088. IEEE.

Flores, C. A., Figueroa, R. L., Pezoa, J. E., and Zeng-Treitler, Q. (2020). CREGEX: A biomedical text classifier based on automatically generated regular expressions. *IEEE Access*, 8:29270–29280.

Goodfellow, I. J., Pouget-Abadie, J., Mirza, M., Xu, B., Warde-Farley, D., Ozair, S., Courville, A., and Bengio, Y. (2014). Generative adversarial networks.

Jofche, N., Mishev, K., Stojanov, R., Jovanovik, M., and Trajanov, D. (2021). Pharmke: Knowledge extraction platform for pharmaceutical texts using transfer learning. *CoRR*, abs/2102.13139.

Lee, J., Yoon, W., Kim, S., Kim, D., Kim, S., So, C. H., and Kang, J. (2020). BioBERT: a pre-trained biomedical language representation model for biomedical text mining. *Bioinform.*, 36(4):1234–1240.

Luo, Y. (2017). Recurrent neural networks for classifying relations in clinical notes. *J. Biomed. Informatics*, 72:85–95.

Reimers, N. and Gurevych, I. (2019). Sentence-BERT: Sentence embeddings using Siamese BERT-networks. In Kentaro Inui, et al., editors, *Proceedings of the 2019 Conference on Empirical Methods in Natural Language Processing and the 9th International Joint Conference on Natural Language Processing, EMNLP-IJCNLP 2019, Hong Kong, China, November 3-7, 2019*, pages 3980–3990. Association for Computational Linguistics.

Sarkar, R., Ojha, A. K., Megaro, J., Mariano, J., Herard, V., and McCrae, J. P. (2021). Few-shot and zero-shot approaches to legal text classification: A case study in the financial sector. In *Proceedings of the Natural Legal Language Processing Workshop 2021*, pages 102–106, Punta Cana, Dominican Republic, November. Association for Computational Linguistics.

Vaswani, A., Shazeer, N., Parmar, N., Uszkoreit, J., Jones, L., Gomez, A. N., Kaiser, L., and Polosukhin, I. (2017). Attention is all you need. In Isabelle Guyon, et al., editors, *Advances in Neural Information Processing Systems 30: Annual Conference on Neural Information Processing Systems 2017, December 4-9, 2017, Long Beach, CA, USA*, pages 5998–6008.

Wu, J., Zhang, R., Gong, T., Liu, Y., Wang, C., and Li, C. (2021). BioIE: Biomedical information extraction with multi-head attention enhanced graph convolutional network. In Yufei Huang, et al., editors, *IEEE International Conference on Bioinformatics and Biomedicine, BIBM 2021, Houston, TX, USA, December 9-12, 2021*, pages 2080–2087. IEEE.

Yao, L., Mao, C., and Luo, Y. (2019). Clinical text classification with rule-based features and knowledge-guided convolutional neural networks. *BMC Medical Informatics Decis. Mak.*, 19-S(3):31–39.

Author Index

Association for Computational Linguistics
209 N. Eighth Street
Stroudsburg, Pennsylvania 18360

ISBN 978-1-7138-6116-4

CURRAN ASSOCIATES INC.
proceedings.com